THE END OF INTERPRETATION

THE END OF INTERPRETATION

Reclaiming the Priority
of Ecclesial Exegesis

R. R. RENO

Ɓ
Baker Academic
a division of Baker Publishing Group
Grand Rapids, Michigan

Published by Baker Academic
a division of Baker Publishing Group
PO Box 6287, Grand Rapids, MI 49516-6287
www.bakeracademic.com

Printed in the United States of America

Library of Congress Cataloging-in-Publication Data
Names: Reno, Russell R., 1959– author.
Title: The end of interpretation : reclaiming the priority of ecclesial exegesis / R. R. Reno.
Description: Grand Rapids, Michigan : Baker Academic, a division of Baker Publishing Group, 2022. | Includes bibliographical references and index.
Identifiers: LCCN 2022004857 | ISBN 9780801096914 (paperback) | ISBN 9781540966124 (casebound) | ISBN 9781493438266 (ebook) | ISBN 9781493438273 (pdf)
Subjects: LCSH: Bible—Criticism, interpretation, etc.
Classification: LCC BS511.3 .R4645 2022 | DDC 220.6—dc23/eng/20220225
LC record available at https://lccn.loc.gov/2022004857

22 23 24 25 26 27 28   7 6 5 4 3 2 1

For Ephraim

CONTENTS

INTRODUCTION

In 1988, then Cardinal Joseph Ratzinger delivered a lecture in New York: "Biblical Interpretation in Crisis." He observed that, after two hundred years of historical-critical study of the Bible, we need "a better synthesis between the historical and theological methods."[1] Achieving this goal requires careful critical thinking about historical criticism, which often claims far greater certainty for its results than closer inspection shows appropriate. And the future Pope Benedict XVI observed that any text—especially sacred Scripture—will give up the full treasure of its meaning only to those who approach with sympathetic hearts open to hearing what is being said rather than with an eagerness to pigeonhole the text in accord with pet ideas and prearranged schemes.

As befits an address by a former theology professor, "Biblical Interpretation in Crisis" was a closely argued lecture. The themes Ratzinger raised remain salient to anyone who wishes to think clearly about the limits (and achievements) of historical criticism and other modern methods of biblical interpretation. Yet the turmoil surrounding his lecture suggests that long-standing

1. Joseph Ratzinger, "Biblical Interpretation in Crisis" (Erasmus Lecture, sponsored by the Institute on Religion and Public Life, New York, NY, 1988), https://www.firstthings.com/web-exclusives/2008/04/biblical-interpretation-in-crisis.

questions concerning hermeneutics, philosophy, and textual methods are secondary in our time, not primary. Ratzinger was then head of the Vatican's Congregation for the Doctrine of the Faith, the office in Rome charged with the task of articulating and enforcing doctrinal standards. Among those standards are moral teachings condemning homosexual acts. As a consequence, his presence in New York attracted gay-rights protesters who disrupted the lecture and, once expelled, banged on the windows. When the lecture was finished, New York police officers had to hustle the cardinal into a nearby police van in order to escape the raucous scene.

Since 1988, the moral hostility toward Christianity has only increased, eclipsing what are now old-fashioned objections that belief in the miraculous and supernatural is not rational or that Christians rely on scriptural testimony that does not stand up to critical scrutiny. In these circumstances, any sort of rapprochement between the standards of academic study and Christian theological commitments, however well argued, gains little traction. A generation ago, it might have been the case that modern historical scholarship could enter into fruitful dialogue with theology. When he became Pope Benedict XVI in 2005, Ratzinger suggested as much. At that time, he returned to the University of Regensburg, where he had served as a professor in the 1970s, and delivered an address to the faculty. He recalled his years there as a professor and expressed his admiration for the seriousness with which both secular and religious scholars discussed matters of consequence from their respective disciplines. Their outlooks were not the same, and disagreements were common. But these learned scholars trusted in their shared commitment to reason, however differently they interpreted its demands.

Today, we sadly hear little of reason. "Wokeness" takes its marching orders from moral certitudes, not from rational inquiry. Appeals to a common commitment to reason do not command assent. As a result, while Ratzinger's call for a better synthesis of faith's understanding and reason's methods remains valid, it makes sense only as an explicitly theological project.

This book presumes that we ought to take great care to honor the truth of our faith, and it is the job of reason, including its modern methods, to purify and deepen that truth. But we must seek this purifying and deepening as Christians.

In my early years of theological study, I was inspired by Karl Barth. His boldness encouraged me to engage other disciplines on theological terms. My teachers were less bombastic than the great Swiss theologian, but in their more measured way they pointed in the same direction. Operating in a Barthian mode (or, as my teachers might say, in a postliberal mode) does not mean theologizing everything. One should read Plato and learn from him. The same can be said for Kant and Hegel, and for Shakespeare and Milton. Hans Urs von Balthasar relished the image of a symphony as a fitting way to picture truth's impress upon our minds. Each instrument must speak in its own voice if it is to be heard in accord with the composer's synthetic genius. The same is true for philosophy, history, science, literature, and every other endeavor. The truth of God in Christ sets the score; theologians do not play each and every instrument.

In the chapters that follow, I discuss historical criticism and on occasion draw upon the insights of modern biblical scholarship. That instrument must be heard. I discuss an ancient Christian figure (Origen), and I do so within the canons of historical scholarship. My aim is to understand him on his own terms, to hear him as he was heard by his contemporaries. Readers may be surprised to discover that in another chapter I give sustained attention to a long Middle English poem. But varied though the instruments may be, the score is unfailingly theological. For these chapters are not organized around the sorts of questions asked by philosophers, historians, or literary critics. Instead, I press theological questions and then turn to many sources as I try to reason my way to satisfactory answers.

Speaking of theological *questions* is not quite right. In truth, this book circles back again and again to a single question: How do we square doctrine with Scripture? This is not a question that university training in biblical studies encourages you to ask. Indeed, as I'll note on a number of occasions in what follows, academic formation actively discourages you from trying to resolve the problem of the Bible's relation to church teaching, deeming it a dangerous temptation, an invitation to impose pious concerns on what should be a purely intellectual investigation.

I do not gainsay a secular scholar's disinterest in the problem of doctrine's relation to Scripture. But let us not be deceived by talk of "purely intellectual enterprises," for it gives the false impression that faith places no demands on reason. As I will show in the pages that follow, squaring doctrine with Scripture is a daunting enterprise, one requiring a wide range of intellectual efforts. In the case of Origen, it motivated an extraordinary and inventive recasting of Neoplatonism. Other early Christian figures drew upon and redeployed ancient theories of rhetoric. And, of course, the church fathers advanced exegetical arguments that are complex and multifaceted. I add my voice to this tradition of reason in service of scriptural interpretation, albeit in a much more limited way, given my lack of scriptural proficiency in comparison to the great figures of the Christian tradition.

Some readers may be disappointed that I forswear preliminary discussions of method and hermeneutics. I do not dig into philosophical material in order to find resources for a theology of interpretation, one that lays out criteria by which we can be assured that our readings and interpretations are reliable, objective, and trustworthy. Nor can one find in these pages a disciplined account of the doctrine of inspiration or any other fully developed theological reflection on Scripture as God's revelation.

As I have gotten older, I've found it best to speak directly about the problems and puzzles that animate our minds rather than first framing these difficulties in rigorous ways. (There is nothing wrong with the writing of prolegomena, other than the danger of failing to get to the matter at hand because one's energies are spent on preliminaries.) After all, the most basic purpose of biblical hermeneutics and relevant methods is to provide satisfactory answers to what is, at bottom, a simple question: How should I interpret so that I remain true to what Scripture says? Across these pages, I repeat on many occasions what I take to be the clearest and most basic answer: proper interpretation proves itself to be such when our reading of Scripture accords with what the church teaches. I detail below how I arrived at this conclusion. But for now, let me simply state it clearly. The imperative of accordance is the first principle of Christian hermeneutics. I strongly encourage readers who are interested in biblical interpretation to read Hans-Georg Gadamer, Paul Ricoeur, and other twentieth-century figures who have subtle and wise things to say about texts, history, and interpretation. I have learned a great deal from them. But I am convinced it is best to get the imperative of accordance clear in our minds before searching for resources and insights useful in elaborating, explaining, and defending our approaches to interpretation.

Ratzinger seems to have come to a similar conclusion. At a session of the 2008 Synod of Bishops, Pope Benedict addressed the participants. It was twenty years after his famous lecture on the crisis of biblical interpretation. He no longer spoke of historical and theological methods. Instead, he framed the challenge of reading the Bible directly: "For the life and mission of the Church, for the future of faith, it is absolutely necessary to overcome the dualism between exegesis and theology."[2] If the truth of our faith is to grow in our hearts and shine brightly into a world in dire need of conversion, we must bring our reading of the Bible into accord with the doctrines that provide an apostolic foundation for our theologies.

2. "Address of His Holiness Benedict XVI during the 14th General Congregation of the Synod of Bishops," October 14, 2008, https://www.vatican.va/content/benedict -xvi/en/speeches/2008/october/documents/hf_ben-xvi_spe_20081014_sinodo.html.

As I shall argue, "overcom[ing] the dualism between exegesis and theology" has been the central Christian project from the beginning. It is manifest every time the New Testament says, ". . . that the Scriptures might be fulfilled." The need to overcome the dualism between a then-conventional reading of the Old Testament and the revelation of God's love in Christ's death and resurrection drives Saint Paul's thinking, giving rise to the many minitreatises of theology in his epistles. "Overcoming" animates the patristic era, and the imperative Pope Benedict identifies is carried forward through the centuries. In this book, I examine a small episode arising from sixteenth-century debates about the doctrine of justification. My own efforts to read the Bible answer to the same task.

The outline of the book is straightforward. The first two chapters lay out the fundamental challenge we face as Christian readers of the Bible, which is to discern the accordance of Scripture with doctrine. I argue that this discerning is what makes interpretation "theological." The problem is easy to see, often painfully so, because Scripture can often seem discordant with church teaching. But we should not be deterred by difficulty. The labor we invest in puzzling our way toward accordance pays rich dividends. Theological exegesis is ambitious and exciting. The imperative of "overcoming" drives us toward insights into the richness of Scripture and the nuances of doctrine, both of which prepare us to receive illuminations from above.

Chapters 3 and 4 provide historical examples of theological interpretation. In Origen we encounter one of the greatest readers in our tradition. He "scripturalized" metaphysics and conceived of a doctrine of inspiration that illuminates the way in which the Bible draws us down the narrow path of sanctification, turning the work of interpretation into a sublime imitation of Christ in his humility and suffering. Reformation-era theologians knew

that they were caught in a vice. On crucial matters of justification, faith, and works, Paul seems to war against James. Scripture speaks against Scripture. These theologians faced rather than
avoided this daunting problem, producing speculative accounts of
the origins and purposes of the Pauline Epistles and the Epistle
of James that foreshadow modern historical insights. The need
to overcome the divide between exegesis and theology not only
drives us closer to God; it also sends us back to a deeper engagement with our predecessors and stimulates our intellects to probe
more deeply—not just into the inner workings of doctrine but
into the meaning of history.

Chapters 5, 6, and 7 present my own exegetical efforts. When
illustrating the nature of theological exegesis in the early chapters,
I make heavy use of my investigations into the first chapter of
Genesis, which I present in more detail in chapter 5. In chapter 6,
I meditate on the theme of Christ's departure in the Gospel of
John, which is paradoxically a way of remaining "at-one" with his
disciples. Chapter 7 illuminates Paul's First Letter to the Corinthians by way of a close reading of *Piers Plowman*, a scripturally
shaped poem written in the late fourteenth century. One often sees
best what a task entails by doing it rather than by falling back on
theory. These are my attempts.

The book ends with reflections on an ambitious project of
performing theological exegesis rather than talking about it: the
Brazos Theological Commentary on the Bible (BTCB). I served as
general editor of this series, contributing my own volume on Genesis (thus explaining my ready recourse to that text in these pages).
My work over the years spent reading and reviewing commentaries
before publication, and working on my own, disabused me of any
notion that putting the word "theological" in front of interpretation implies a distinct method. The remarkable—nay, extreme—
heterogeneity of the series forced me to think more clearly about
church-oriented, theologically informed exegesis. This ultimately
led me to the first principle of Christian hermeneutics: the best

reading of Scripture discerns its concordance with doctrine. From that principle this book arises.

———

As I note in my discussion of the first verse of Genesis, "beginning" has a variety of meanings. Fear of the Lord is the beginning of wisdom, we are told. That use of beginning signifies the foundation or basis of wisdom rather than its origin in time. The same meaning of beginning holds for the role that the imperative of accordance between Scripture and doctrine—the "overcoming" that Pope Benedict urges—plays in this volume. It serves as this book's basis, rationale, and purpose. Temporality is another matter. Most of the following chapters are based on essays and lectures written in the first decade of this century, during my tenure as a professor of theology. (See the acknowledgments at the end of the book.) Over the past decade, my day job has taken me out of my former vocation as an academic theologian. A great deal of my attention is now spent thinking and writing about the ephemeral affairs of men and women struggling in the political and cultural battles of our time. But throughout the 2010s, Dave Nelson at Baker Academic, my editorial coworker on the Brazos Theological Commentary on the Bible series, kept prodding me to publish this material. Fearing that I would be like the dogs of the Bible that return to their vomit, I resisted. In the end, Dave prevailed.

When I reread what I had written about theological interpretation, I was dissatisfied. Every element had to be substantially revised. I set to work, at first with grim determination, but over time with greater and greater pleasure. It is a blessing to work in the vineyard of God's ever-fruitful Word. I hope that you, dear reader, will sip from the same cup of gladness.

WHAT MAKES EXEGESIS THEOLOGICAL?

I SERVED AS THE EDITOR of the Brazos Theological Commentary on the Bible series for more than a decade. On the basis of that experience I can confidently report that there is no danger of a precisely formulated, rigorously implemented "theological method" emerging. The approaches, techniques, and interpretive strategies employed by the commentators in the Brazos series have been extraordinarily diverse, almost maddeningly so. In the first published commentary, Jaroslav Pelikan worked his way through the Acts of the Apostles, often highlighting verses that invite extended theological reflection.[1] For example, Pelikan uses Acts 12:7 ("Suddenly an angel of the Lord appeared [to Peter]") as the occasion to discuss angels in the canon as a whole. (I adopted a somewhat similar approach in my commentary on Genesis.)[2] In a volume published soon thereafter, Telford Work commented on a much larger number of individual verses in Deuteronomy, using

---

1. Jaroslav Pelikan, *Acts*, BTCB (Grand Rapids: Brazos, 2005). The series went on to publish more than 20 volumes.
2. R. R. Reno, *Genesis*, BTCB (Grand Rapids: Brazos, 2010).

an inventive format that organized his largely anagogical commentary in accord with the theological virtues of faith, hope, and love.[3] Peter Leithart and others commented chapter by chapter.[4] Others parsed biblical books in different ways.

Nevertheless, readers and reviewers of the Brazos series sense a unity of purpose, if not execution. As I sought to explain in my general introduction to the series, the basic premise of the Brazos Theological Commentary on the Bible is that the Nicene tradition plays an indispensable role in good biblical interpretation. Just what counts as the Nicene tradition is very much a matter of debate, and the precise role dogma plays in exegesis resists definition. But the larger claim is, I think, accessible to our understanding. Bringing classical Christian teaching to bear in scriptural analysis and exposition will conduce to saying something helpful and true about the biblical text. "Theological interpretation" has emerged as the imprecise but nonetheless useful term to designate a doctrinally informed approach.

This admittedly vague description tends to evoke pressing questions from anxious biblical scholars. Won't employing dogma in the exegetical process turn biblical exposition into a parochial enterprise at best, or a stultifying fundamentalism at worst? Why give up on the confessional neutrality that secures a place for biblical studies in the secular university? And don't we need an objective approach to the Bible precisely so that we can find a reliable scriptural basis for doctrine and theology, protecting the Bible from being turned into a wax nose easily molded to serve confessional agendas?

These are important questions. But I want to set them aside for the moment in order to address a more fundamental concern. Why do we feel a need to have something called "theological" exegesis in the first place? Isn't well-informed and thoughtful biblical

3. Telford Work, *Deuteronomy*, BTCB (Grand Rapids: Brazos, 2009).
4. Peter J. Leithart, *1 & 2 Kings*, BTCB (Grand Rapids: Brazos, 2006).

interpretation what we want, whatever its stated methods? What work does the adjective "theological" do, aside from picking unnecessary fights with modern biblical scholars?

Calling an approach to Scripture "theological" is a novelty, and a quite recent one at that. In *The Life of Moses*, Gregory of Nyssa identifies two exegetical tasks. The first involves laying out for the reader what he calls the history (*historia*). The interpreter needs to establish the order and sequence of events recounted in the biblical text. The second and more important task requires discerning the spiritual meaning that draws the mind toward contemplation of divine things. Gregory calls this meaning *theōria*. During the Middle Ages, a fourfold scheme was established, and the Bible was read in accord with its literal, allegorical, moral, and anagogical senses. The first is akin to Gregory's notion of *historia*. The interpreter clarifies grammatical ambiguities and resolves tensions in the chronology of events, as well as other difficulties. The latter three are modes of spiritual interpretation. The moral sense edifies, and the anagogical sense addresses our final destiny. The allegorical sense is more open ended. It concerns symbols, patterns, and figures in Scripture that point elsewhere. (*Allegory* is a compound of Greek words that joins "other" with "speaking," and so the literal meaning of *allegory* is "other speaking.") Within this medieval tradition many disputes erupted, especially concerning the possibility and limits of allegorical interpretation, which is sometimes restricted to Old Testament typologies that point toward fulfillment in Christ. But whatever our judgments about the old tradition of the fourfold sense of Scripture, we must be honest: the term "theological" is not used.

Nor was the locution "theological exegesis" or its analogues employed by early modern figures such as George Horne (1730–1792), whose popular commentary on the Psalms self-consciously opposed the historical-critical methods that were already being developed in the eighteenth century.[5] William Temple did not use the term "theological" to describe his extraordinary commentary on the Gospel of John, which he published in the late 1930s. He allows that elements of his *Readings in St. John's Gospel* might be called "a series of devotional meditations," but he insists that his approach "has no distinctive and consistent character." The most Temple was willing to say is that he followed the text where it led him, "and I hope that this is not totally different from saying that I am concerned with what the Holy Spirit says to me through the Gospel."[6]

Although I have not done extensive research, I have the distinct impression that the term "theological exegesis" emerged during the final decades of the twentieth century. George Lindbeck framed the notion in "The Story-Shaped Church: Critical Exegesis and Theological Interpretation," his contribution to a 1987 volume honoring his Yale colleague Hans Frei.[7] In that dense essay, Lindbeck argues that our theology of the church, while expressed in terms drawn from Scripture, is not always evidently "scriptural" in the strict sense of resting on close analysis of particular biblical passages with obvious relevance to church life. Rather, the church's self-understanding turns on efforts to be faithful to the canon within the canon, which (as Lindbeck notes) Hans Frei identified as the composite story that emerges from the four Gospel accounts of the person and work of Jesus of Nazareth.

Lindbeck develops his argument within carefully circumscribed parameters. He limits his remarks to the doctrine of the church, especially insofar as it draws upon the Old Testament account of the people of Israel. But I can state his conclusion more generally.

5. *A Commentary on the Book of the Psalms* was first published in 1776. It has been republished many times and remains in print to this day.

6. *Readings in St. John's Gospel* was published in two phases, the First Series (1939) and the Second Series (1940). My volume combined both and was published by Macmillan, 1955. Temple's characterization of his approach can be found on page ix.

7. Garrett Green, ed., *Scriptural Authority and Narrative Interpretation* (Philadelphia: Fortress, 1987), 161–78.

Close attention to the history of the church shows that the church's teaching, preaching, and practice are not "derived" from Scripture. They arise from an always-ongoing act of scriptural interpretation that seeks to correlate specific biblical passages with present concerns and imperatives. One sees this process at work in *Four Discourses against the Arians*, the extended polemic against Arianism penned by Athanasius. The bulk of this defense of the divinity of Christ involves detailed exegesis. Like so many others in the early centuries of Christian history, the treatise features page after page of biblical interpretation guided by a powerful although rarely theorized "christological" sense of what Scripture as a whole reveals.

David Yeago was a student of George Lindbeck. Yeago's 1993 essay "The New Testament and the Nicene Dogma: A Contribution to the Recovery of Theological Exegesis" provides another instance of the use of "theological" as the fitting adjective for a churchly approach to the Bible.[8] Yeago observes that premodern theologians may not have agreed with one another about doctrine, but they universally presumed that orthodox dogma expresses the teaching of Scripture. In the modern era this presumption was overturned. Classical doctrines were taken to be ersatz philosophical speculation imposed upon the biblical text—the Greek mind at work, not the Hebraic logic of Scripture, as German scholars liked to say in the late nineteenth and early twentieth centuries. Protestant pietism reinforced this tendency. It encouraged an experiential approach rather than one guided by doctrine, which was thought to promote a dry religious rationalism. According to the pietist, the Bible's true sense sparks warm feelings of an intimate relation to God. The great German theologian of the modern era Friedrich Schleiermacher (1768–1834) theorized this approach in terms congenial to the intellectual currents of Romanticism. Soon thereafter, Protestant faculties (especially in

8. David Yeago, "The New Testament and the Nicene Dogma: A Contribution to the Recovery of Theological Exegesis," *Pro Ecclesia* 3, no. 2 (1993): 152–64.

Germany) adopted the new methods of historical criticism, which were championed as the only reliable way to determine what the Bible "really means." All these factors contributed to the modern Christian predicament. The close connection between doctrine and Scripture was undone.

It's wrong to imagine that historical criticism alone bears the blame. Even as the authority of that method recedes, the notion remains widespread that theology is best understood as religiously inspired philosophy rather than the distillation of the church's exegetical tradition. One can easily imagine a theology graduate student reading Emmanuel Levinas and writing a dissertation about the Trinity as the incorporation of "the other" into the eternal life of God. The experiential emphasis remains strong as well, although these days it is often given a moralizing twist. Jesus encourages an empathic affirmation of the stranger, we are told. Or he inculcates in us revolutionary ardor and stokes a commitment to overturning unjust structures. It was against these trends that Lindbeck and Yeago brandished the term "theological exegesis." They were seeking to recover an earlier consensus, one that saw the church's doctrines and liturgies as arising out of sound exegesis and that therefore trusted that those doctrines and liturgies train us to read the Bible well.

There is also a historical claim about "theological exegesis" in Lindbeck's and Yeago's arguments. It holds that premodern churchmen engaged in a vast, never-ending project of using doctrine to interpret Scripture and Scripture to illuminate doctrine. Out of this project emerges a biblically saturated worldview, an extraordinary web of philosophical speculation, historical assessment, and moral exhortation through which run golden threads of biblical language. However defective in this detail or that specific respect, the exegetically spun web was sound. "Theological interpretation" is not, therefore, a method. It marks a decision by today's readers to trust in the scriptural genesis and biblical genius of the church's traditions.

So we return to the questions many biblical scholars have raised about theological interpretation. Are we to renounce the insights of historical understanding and descend into fundamentalism? Will we end up reading our theologies into Scripture rather than allowing Scripture to inform and govern our theologies? To answer these questions, I need to make the case for a striking claim: Christians have no choice but to embrace an approach of the sort suggested by Lindbeck and Yeago. By making this case I hope to illuminate the concept of theological exegesis more fully. With this deeper understanding, we can return to the objections and concerns expressed by often friendly but anxious critics and provide some responses.

———

Let's begin with the simple and rather obvious claim that the true church of Jesus Christ teaches the gospel of Jesus Christ. This affirmation leads to what I call "the presumption of accordance." If the Bible teaches something we judge integral to the gospel, then we hold that the church's teaching must be substantially the same. The reverse holds as well. If the church teaches something as a saving truth, then we assume that the Bible does so. It's that simple: what the Bible says accords with what the church proclaims.

This presumption seems hard to swallow. Let me therefore state the case for accordance more precisely. Given our assumption that the true church of Christ teaches the gospel of Christ as witnessed to by Scripture, we presume that our exegesis of the Bible ought to line up nicely with what we take to be orthodox doctrine. And if this turns out not to be the case (and discordance certainly happens), we conclude either that our interpretations are wrongheaded or that what we imagine to be orthodox doctrine is not, in fact, orthodox. I see no third possibility for the faithful Christian. One way or another, true doctrine and sound exegesis must be in accordance.

But what about church teachings that are not found in the Bible? The Catholic Church, for example, elaborates principles for just war, declares life to begin at conception, and prohibits the use of artificial methods of birth control. None of these teachings are found in the Bible, at least not directly so. The Catholic Church recognizes the lack of direct scriptural foundations, describing these doctrines as the results of reason properly applied to moral issues rather than as revealed truths. Or take the dogmatic affirmations of the Immaculate Conception and the Bodily Assumption of Mary. Church documents that define these dogmas appeal to passages in Scripture, but the dogmas are not biblical in a strict sense, at least not in ways that satisfy most Protestants. Again, the Catholic Church recognizes this to be the case. Treatises defending the doctrines of the Immaculate Conception and the Bodily Assumption usually rely on theories of magisterial authority and the development of doctrine to justify their apostolic authenticity.

Nevertheless, a well-catechized Catholic holds that these and other teachings of the Church accord with the larger sweep of biblical revelation. As I'll demonstrate at length as we go along, the first chapter of Genesis and the prologue to the Gospel of John indicate that God creates with his Word, which means creation has a *logos*, an order. The Catholic tradition (and other Christian traditions as well) holds that reason can know this order in the form of natural law. This presumption finds scriptural support. The book of Proverbs testifies to the existence of natural law, as do other portions of the Bible. The same appeal to the larger witness of Scripture holds for the doctrine of the Immaculate Conception of Mary, which draws upon Old Testament accounts of the tabernacle in which the divine presence dwells. The doctrine of the Bodily Assumption of Mary fulfills Jesus's promise, "There are some standing here who will not taste death" (Matt. 16:28), and Job's testimony, "In my flesh I shall see God" (Job 19:26).

These brief suggestions do not do justice to the arguments in favor of these Catholic doctrines. Making the full case would require long treatises. But I do not aim to convince readers. I wish only to point out that Catholic affirmations of these doctrines and teachings presume that they accord with Scripture. Even the Catholic affirmations of magisterial authority—the claim that Marian doctrines are apostolic because declared to be so by the church—reflect an appeal to Scripture, for the Catholic case for the church's authority is buttressed by many exegetical arguments showing the primacy of Peter.

This persistent recourse to Scripture should not surprise us. No matter how we conceptualize or articulate the authority of biblical revelation, no matter what sort of ecclesiology we employ to describe the apostolic character of the church, nearly all Christians adopt the presumption of accordance. We take it for granted that the supreme trustworthiness of Scripture as the Word of God dovetails with the church's doctrine and teaching, liturgical practice, and moral exhortation. Revelation and proclamation need to be on the same page, as it were.

The presumption of accordance operates openly in the confessional traditions of the churches in the West. The Council of Trent, for example, juxtaposes the evils of personal judgment (which they accused Protestants of employing) to the proper path of interpretation guided by "holy mother Church." For the bishops at Trent, it was intolerable that private persons should set about to produce readings of the Bible contrary to those established by the traditions of the church. Therefore, to prevent the possibility of disjunctions between biblical interpretation and church teaching, the council formulated a crucial post-Reformation definition of magisterial authority. It is the prerogative of the church, we read, "to judge of the true sense and interpretation of the holy Scriptures."[9] This assertion of ecclesiastical authority over our interpretations of the Bible has a clear purpose—it secures accordance.

9. "General Council of Trent: Fourth Session," ed. and trans. J. Waterworth, Papal Encyclicals Online, "Decree concerning the Edition, and the Use, of the Sacred Books," https://www.papalencyclicals.net/councils/trent/fourth-session.htm.

The First and Second Vatican Councils reiterate the same concept of magisterial authority. Vatican I's "Dogmatic Constitution
on the Catholic Faith" (*Dei Filius*) makes this declaration:

> Now since the decree on the interpretation of holy scripture, prof-
> itably made by the council of Trent, with the intention of con-
> straining rash speculation, has been wrongly interpreted by some,
> we renew that decree and declare its meaning to be as follows:
> that in matters of faith and morals, belonging as they do to the
> establishing of christian doctrine, that the meaning of holy scrip-
> ture must be held to be the true one, which holy mother church
> held and holds, since it is her right to judge the true meaning and
> interpretation of holy scripture.[10]

The Second Vatican Council's "Dogmatic Constitution on Divine
Revelation" (*Dei Verbum*) provides a more extensive, plastic, and
complex account of the role and interpretation of Scripture in
the life of the church. In an important correction to earlier formulations, which give the impression that the magisterium has an
authority higher than Scripture, Vatican II states, "This teaching
office is not above the word of God, but serves it, teaching only
what has been handed on, listening to it devoutly, guarding it
scrupulously and explaining it faithfully in accord with a divine
commission and with the help of the Holy Spirit."[11] Nevertheless,

10. "Decrees of the First Vatican Council," Papal Encyclicals Online, Session 3,
"Dogmatic Constitution on the Catholic Faith," *Dei Filius*, chapter 2, https://www
.papalencyclicals.net/councils/ecum20.htm. The restatement and clarification of Trent
was motivated by concerns about two nineteenth-century opinions, both of which
sought to loosen the bond between church teaching and scriptural interpretation.
One argued that Trent's decree was purely disciplinary and not dogmatic in consequence. The second argued that Trent required assent to dogmas officially derived
from Scripture but not assent to the particular interpretations. For background, see
Jean-Michel-Alfred Vacant, *Études théologiques sur les constitutions du Concile de
Vatican*, Tome 1 (Paris: Delhomme et Briguet, 1895), 520–21.
11. Vatican II, "Dogmatic Constitution on Divine Revelation," *Dei Verbum* (The
Holy See: Web Archive), sec. 10, https://www.vatican.va/archive/hist_councils/ii
_vatican_council/documents/vat-ii_const_19651118_dei-verbum_en.html.

the assertion of exegetical authority remains intact: "The task of authentically interpreting the word of God . . . has been entrusted exclusively to the living teaching office of the Church, whose authority is exercised in the name of Jesus Christ."[12]

One can mount endless objections to the Catholic approach to biblical interpretation, judging it to be authoritarian, anti-historical, unscriptural, and so forth. Yet we must acknowledge that Catholicism presumes accordance. By clearly stipulating that the church and only the church rightly judges the meaning of Scripture, the Catholic Church seeks to ensure what nearly all Christians assume to be the case: a tight fit between what the church teaches and what the Bible says.

Protestant confessional documents reject many Catholic doctrines, but not the presumption of accordance. The Lutheran Formula of Concord opens with the Protestant principle of *sola scriptura*. "We believe, teach, and confess," the formula states, "that the only rule and guiding principle according to which all teachings and teachers are to be evaluated and judged are the prophetic and apostolic writings of the Old and New Testaments alone."[13] In the Reformed tradition, the Westminster Confession emphasizes the necessity of the illumination of the Holy Spirit, as well as a place for natural reason in practical considerations of church order. But the basic principle remains the same: "The Supreme Judge, by which all controversies of religion are to be determined, and all decrees of councils, opinions of ancient writers, doctrines of men, and private spirits, are to be examined, and in whose sentence we are to rest, can be no other but the Holy Spirit speaking in the Scripture."[14]

12. Vatican II, "Dogmatic Constitution on Divine Revelation," *Dei Verbum*, sec. 10.

13. Formula of Concord, Epitome 1, in *The Book of Concord: The Confessions of the Evangelical Lutheran Church*, ed. Robert Kolb and Timothy J. Wengert (Minneapolis: Fortress, 2000).

14. Westminster Confession of Faith 1.10, in *The Constitution of the Presbyterian Church (U.S.A.): Part 1, Book of Confessions*, 145–202 (Louisville: Office of

Reformation documents start on the opposite side, empha-
sizing the authority of Scripture rather than that of the church.
But these foundational Protestant confessional statements end up
affirming the presumption of accordance of doctrine and Scripture, as does the Council of Trent and the two modern Vatican
Councils. Lutherans and Calvinists insist that what the church
teaches must line up with what the Bible says, while Catholics
say that what we take the Bible to be saying must be in line with
what the church teaches. The two sides of the great Reformation
debates about church authority and *sola scriptura* differ greatly
on the question of whether to start with biblical interpretation
or church authority (although that difference may not be as great
as advertised, as the Missouri Synod Lutheran tradition of dis-
couraging Bible reading unsupervised by the pastor indicates).
But let's set aside that important difference so that we can see an
even more important agreement: Protestants and Catholics agree
that the true meaning of the Bible and the church's proclamation
testify to the self-same truth.

The presumption of accordance is so primitive to Christian
identity that even aggressively nonconfessional, "Bible only"
Protestants endorse it. Nondenominational Bible churches reject
the instrumentalities of written confessions, insisting that Scripture alone must be the criterion of truth. They regard creeds to
be man-made documents that stand in the way of the complete
correspondence between scriptural interpretation and church
teaching. We should not embark on two different enterprises,
they argue, one that interprets the Bible and another that formulates doctrines. The two should be one and the same in godly
"Bible preaching." And so we see that, yes, there are bitter debates about church authority, confessional documents, theories
of inerrancy, or methods of interpretation. But from the most
ultramontane Catholics to the most anticonfessional Protestants,

the General Assembly, 2016), https://www.pcusa.org/site_media/media/uploads/oga
/pdf/boc2016.pdf.

the presumption of accordance is not itself controversial. It is instead the great point of agreement around which theological controversies swirl.

Which brings us back to the notion of theological exegesis as outlined by Lindbeck and Yeago. It is an approach to Scripture that does nothing more than presume what nearly all Christians presume: what the church teaches accords with what the Bible says. This presumption does not rule out historical questions any more than it rules out philosophical ones. But it does establish a criterion for biblical interpretation. Put simply, if we think that what our churches teach is correct, then no matter how wide ranging our research and diverse our methods, we must conduct our interpretive work under the assumption that a correct reading of the Bible, while it may not confirm every detail, accords with doctrine. And if we can't discern at least a modicum of accordance, then we know we have a problem to solve. Either we need to return to our exegesis and puzzle again about the meaning of the passage we are interpreting, or we need to read up on theology and church history so that we can be sure we understand aright the church's doctrines.

I can feel the reader's unhappiness. I have explained the presumption of accordance in a number of academic and church settings. Invariably I meet resistance. Shouldn't our interpretation be objective, not under dogmatic control? Don't we want exegetes to operate freely, following the biblical text where it leads rather than working with "presumptions"? Isn't this agenda regressive, taking us back to premodern times when church authorities tried to exercise a stultifying control over academic inquiry into history? And so on, and so on, sometimes late into the night.

It's worth pondering the urgency we feel when it comes to questions of biblical interpretation, an urgency that gives rise to great anxiety about methods of interpretation. People don't raise their voices in debates about how to interpret Shakespeare. Intense

conflicts over exegesis of the *Iliad* do not implicate the faith of
millions of people, as did the great contest over scriptural authority in the Southern Baptist Convention in the 1980s. There is no
Bart Ehrman who writes books designed to show Jane Austen fans
that they have been brought up to misinterpret the great novelist.
We should not be surprised by these differences, for the Bible is
not just any book. It has authority, not just for the over two billion
Christians worldwide but for the culture of the West, for which it
was the book of books until only recently. With so much at stake,
it is difficult to think clearly.

But we must try.

Let me stipulate a noncontroversial principle of reason: we
should use what is clear in order to understand what is obscure.
We don't exercise ourselves to interpret easy texts. Their meaning
seems evident; they speak for themselves. But when we're not sure
about something, we must bring our uncertainties into the light of
our certainties. To be less dogmatic, we frame what we're not sure
about in terms of what we're more confident about. For example,
if we're quite sure that God does not exist, we'll naturally interpret
the Bible in purely historical terms, reading the Old Testament as
the cultural-political project of ancient Israelite religion, a project
that seeks to legitimate priestly and royal power. Or if we think
patriarchy defines history, then a certain kind of feminist interpretation of the Bible makes sense. The same holds for postcolonial
and other readings. With these approaches, interpreters are using
what to their minds is self-evident in order to interpret a very
old, often confusing text—the Bible. Say what you want about
secularist, feminist, or postcolonialist assumptions, but you need
to acknowledge that using the clear to illuminate the obscure is
normal procedure.

The self-same procedure guides theological interpretation, but
with an important difference. Unlike historical-critical, feminist,
and other approaches, a theologically informed reading has no
"method." Church doctrine is not a collection of Cartesian ideas

that enjoy adamantine clarity. On the contrary, the church teaches many things in many different ways. Some doctrines are defined in creeds; some are adumbrated in liturgies; still other doctrines find expression in the ongoing stream of preaching and instruction. Like Scripture, the church's teaching is old and often confusing as well. For this reason, the presumption of accordance does not encourage a wooden, formulaic approach. The opposite is the case. It requires extraordinary mobility of mind. There are times when doctrine is far from clear, while the Bible speaks with remarkable directness. Compare, for example, the chiseled clarity of Jesus's statements about his relation to the Father in the Gospel of John with the subtle and difficult concepts used to expound the doctrine of the Trinity. In this instance, we are invited to use Scripture to illuminate doctrine, not doctrine to interpret Scripture.

At other times, doctrine seems to contradict Scripture. In these cases, unlike with modern methods, the presumption of accordance prevents the theological interpreter from jumping to the conclusion that either Scripture or doctrine must be wrong. We are called to a deeper engagement. I felt this demand when I wrote my commentary on Genesis. (I'll have much more to say on this topic in chapter 5, "In the Beginning.") At the very outset there appears to be a striking contrast between what the Bible says and what the church teaches. In Genesis 1:2 we read: "The earth was a formless void and darkness covered the face of the deep, while a wind from God swept over the face of the waters." Some modern biblical scholars give detailed accounts of the connections between this verse and the Babylonian creation myth, Enuma Elish. On the strength of these connections, scholars conclude that in its original context Genesis was read as teaching that God tamed or formed a preexisting chaos. But doctrine says otherwise. Both Jews and Christians have long agreed that God creates out of nothing, *creatio ex nihilo*. Given the presumption of accordance, the problem is obvious. What the Bible seems to say in

Genesis 1:2 and what the church teaches are discordant rather than
harmonious.

Sometimes contradictions really are contradictions. But sometimes further research and reflection show otherwise. In my own
work, I was driven to question my assumptions. I had unthinkingly
assumed that the creation account in Genesis was the source of
the classical doctrine of creation, but modern historical-critical
interpretation suggests that this is not the case. But if the first
verses of Genesis do not provide support for the doctrine of creation out of nothing, how is it that ancient Jews and Christians
came to teach it? The presumption of accordance blocks the easy
conclusion, so common among modern readers, that the church's
teaching is unscriptural. I had to apply myself to the exegetical
task with redoubled effort.

My first step was to make sure I actually understood the doctrine of *creatio ex nihilo*. For help I turned to Robert Sokolowski's
book *The God of Faith and Reason*.[15] This led to the discovery
that the main thrust of the doctrine is metaphysical: there is *nothing* other than the one true God and all the things he has made.
Put somewhat differently, the doctrine of creation out of nothing
promotes what might be called "ontological parsimony." When it
comes to reality, Christians and Jews are stingy. They limit divine
reality to God while according a strict finitude to created reality.
This parsimony stands in contrast to the rococo Neoplatonic view
that allows for many layers and degrees of reality emanating from
the singular divine source.

With the notion of ontological parsimony in mind, I returned to
the Bible and discovered that the extensive Old Testament polemic
against idolatry was the true scriptural basis for the doctrine of
creation out of nothing. Idols are not weak, ineffective, or inadequate; they are empty and lifeless. "Idols are like scarecrows,"

15. Robert Sokolowski, *The God of Faith and Reason: Foundations of Christian
Theology* (Washington, DC: Catholic University of America Press, 1995).

we read in Jeremiah; "they cannot do evil, nor is it in them to do good" (Jer. 10:5). The New Testament carries forward the same view. Saint Paul explains the futility of idols by appealing to God's creative uniqueness (Acts 14:15; 17:24). Idols are futile and vacant, as they must be, for the ontological parsimony of the doctrine of creation out of nothing denies the existence of intermediary, semi-divine realities that might infuse them with power. This is why Paul remains undisturbed by the fact that some of the faithful are eating meat sacrificed to idols; they have no malignant potency (1 Cor. 8:4–6). Given the larger biblical witness, it's therefore natural that idolatry should be the issue at stake in 2 Maccabees 7:28, the only Old Testament passage (in the Catholic Bible) in which creation out of nothing is explicitly affirmed.

And in the development of the doctrine of *creatio ex nihilo* I discovered more than the central role of the biblical campaign against idolatry. Ontological parsimony bears on a wide array of issues. The cogency of the Bible's accounts of divine action in history seems to require the metaphysical assumptions we find in the doctrine of creation out of nothing. The same holds for the unexpected unity of God's universal purposes with the particularity of human history that begins with the calling of Abraham and reaches a crescendo in John 1:14 ("And the Word became flesh and lived among us").[16]

With the fresh insight I had gained into the sources and implications of *creatio ex nihilo*, I was able to return to Genesis 1:2 with a more vivid sense of what is at stake. I saw for the first time a connection between this verse and an Augustinian understanding of the dissolving, destroying, negating, and evacuating power of evil. This view of evil as nothingness allows us to hear the divine pronouncement "Let there be light" (Gen. 1:3) as a word of redemption that echoes in Deuteronomy, where again and again

---

16. See Sokolowski, *God of Faith and Reason*, 31–40. See also book 1 of *Against Heresies*, where Irenaeus makes the doctrine of creation the focus of his refutation of Gnostic views of salvation.

Moses exhorts the Israelites to choose life instead of death. And the link between light and life is made explicit in the Gospel of John. Christ is light and life, and he is with God "in the beginning," laying the deepest foundations of creation.

I could give many more examples from my exegetical efforts, as well as from those undertaken by others as they wrote their commentaries in the Brazos Theological Commentary on the Bible series. When Genesis 17:7 stipulates that the covenant of circumcision will be everlasting, a Christian reader immediately thinks of Galatians 5:2, where Paul says, "If you let yourselves be circumcised, Christ will be of no benefit to you." Here we find two relatively clear scriptural passages that are difficult to harmonize. This motivated me to try to explain how the Pauline rejection of circumcision is consistent with an affirmation of its everlasting role in God's plan of salvation. It is an explanation that involves a fair amount of theologizing.[17] Or take an example from Robert Jenson's commentary on Ezekiel, also in the Brazos series. At the end of Ezekiel 22, we read that God is attacking Jerusalem and at the same time searching for a righteous man to stand in the breach and defend the city against the divinely orchestrated assault. It seems hopelessly confusing. Is God outside the walls of the city pressing his attack? Or is he inside, seeking to save his beloved people? This double role is not so much resolved as made clear and explicit, Jenson suggests, in the crucifixion and resurrection of Christ, in which God is both judge and judged.[18]

My point is not to argue for the cogency of these interpretations. Perhaps they are wrongheaded. Or they perhaps stretch too far—or don't stretch far enough. The adequacy of these readings is for others to judge. Rather, my purpose is to illustrate some of the ways in which the presumption of accordance motivates a mobile and plastic exegesis rather than imposing prepackaged

17. Reno, *Genesis*, 173–80.
18. Robert W. Jenson, *Ezekiel*, BTCB (Grand Rapids: Brazos, 2009), 188.

interpretations onto Scripture. Apparent clashes between doctrine and Scripture frame exciting interpretive questions. The clarity of Scripture can illuminate the mysteries of the faith as defined by doctrine, while at other times classical dogma can point the way toward resolution of what seem like intractable intra-scriptural contradictions.

Again, my goal right now is not to defend any particular exegetical arguments. My point is that the central affirmation of theological exegesis—the presumption of accordance—is fruitful, not stultifying. As we allow church teaching and biblical proclamation to share in a common claim to truth, the obvious differences and puzzling divergences will naturally compel our minds and draw us to construct arguments that interweave theological and biblical analysis. This weaving is exactly the enterprise that Lindbeck and Yeago argue has shaped the Christian tradition from the outset.

All efforts of interpretation try to say something true about the text under examination, which is the reason why our traditions adopt the presumption of accordance. Of course, those truths need not be theological. They can be philological, text-critical, form-critical, historical, moral, or political. But one way or another, we undertake our interpretations against the background of an economy of truth. That economy can be limited and particular in scope. We pursue philological analysis under guiding assumptions about how grammar works and languages evolve—an economy of linguistic truth, as it were. These assumptions are decisive for a philologist. But they are not all-encompassing. For example, I doubt that the arguments in the area of Hebrew philology change much whether one is an ancient Platonist, medieval Aristotelian, or modern-day empiricist.

Metaphysical agnosticism diminishes as we develop larger-scale interpretive arguments. The ambitious speculations of modern historical criticism draw upon often unspoken assumptions about the ways in which human history and culture unfold. For example, the J and P hypothesis in modern interpretation of the Old Testament enjoys a great deal of important and compelling support in the textual details of the Pentateuch, especially in the different locutions used to refer to God (Yahweh versus Elohim). By my reckoning, the existence of J (Yahweh) and P (Elohim) and other textual strands in the first five books of the Bible cannot be denied. But modern scholars do more than that. They use redaction criticism (speculation about the conditions under which the texts were composed and combined in an editing process) to speculate about the significance of the intermingled J and P strands. This approach depends upon theories of tradition and historical development, and these theories depend upon an implicit metaphysics. The role of a metaphysical horizon in interpretation is even more explicit when New Testament scholars stipulate that they must presume that miracles and prophecies cannot happen. This presumption is blatantly metaphysical, for it stipulates what *can* and *cannot* happen. And it leads them to conclude that reports in the Gospels of Jesus's prophecies of the destruction of the temple were composed after the fact, providing decisive evidence for authorship after AD 70.

Trying to interpret any text without recourse to a metaphysical horizon is like trying to walk without legs or see without eyes. For the most part, we are untroubled by the necessity of background assumption. For example, a seminar on *The Protocols of the Elders of Zion* might attempt to discern the reasons for and methods of that text's composition, and to assess its influence. These approaches promise interesting insights into anti-Semitism and the machinations of a modern police state, to say nothing of the perversions of the human heart. A good professor knows how to bring out these insights by framing questions and interpretations in light of an economy of truth. Perhaps the professor presumes certain things about human motivations, fears, and fantasies. Or perhaps he appeals to truths about the larger sweep of modern history or to truths about our common humanity. Students appreciate this sort of class, and books written in this way attract grateful readers. We want a larger horizon that helps us see how a book such as *The Protocols of the Elders of Zion*, which is full of falsehoods, can nonetheless illuminate and refine our insights into what *is* true.

With texts we hold dear, we become more anxious about the role of our assumptions. Although we may want to understand and interpret *The Protocols of the Elders of Zion*, we don't want to adopt its worldview. We want to understand the text, but we don't want to be influenced by it. As a consequence, we worry very little about whether our assumptions about truth control our reading. The situation changes somewhat when we read Shakespeare. Because we think his plays rich with insights into the human condition, we want our minds to be influenced by his work. We don't just want to know about Shakespeare or to understand him in light of our assumptions about culture, history, and the human condition. We also want to think with Shakespeare when we interpret *Macbeth* or *King Lear*. We want our horizon of truth to be open to challenge and perhaps modification.

I call this approach one of interpretive submission, even obedience. We are happy to place *The Protocols of the Elders of Zion* within our economy of truth. But we want Shakespeare's plays to influence our assumptions about truth. The importance of submission becomes acute when a reader approaches the Bible as the Word of God. The doctrines of inspiration and inerrancy affirm that the Bible offers a supreme, comprehensive, and transcendent wisdom. Scripture provides the master code for all reality, and faithful interpreters rightly want their economy of truth to be biblical. Put simply, as faithful Christians we would like to have some confidence that the metaphysical horizon we use to frame our interpretations of the Bible is itself biblical in substance.

In this regard, whether or not they do so explicitly, most Christians affirm the principle of *sola scriptura*. For example, many

modern biblical scholars who wish to function as Christian exegetes appeal to the doctrine of the incarnation as a warrant for
their historical analysis. They are staking a claim to a biblical basis
for the modern, historicist horizon of truth that usually provides
the background assumptions for historical-critical study of the Bible.[19] In my estimation, this use of the doctrine of the incarnation
to justify the historicist assumptions of modern historical criticism
fails to persuade. But the impulse is sound. As I have shown in
this chapter, the presumption of accordance encourages us to have
a great deal of confidence in the biblical substance of orthodox
doctrine. And rightly so. As Lindbeck and Yeago point out, the
Nicene tradition arose from an extended exegetical engagement
with the Old and New Testaments. This means that church doctrine and its metaphysical assumptions may not be perfect and
beyond reform, but they are always already biblically saturated.

Consider, for example, On First Principles, which was the first
sustained Christian effort of speculative, systematic theology. (I
will have a great deal more to say about Origen in chapter 3.) At
the outset of this work, Origen states that his approach has "no
other source but the very words and teachings of Christ."[20] If we
allow ourselves to become bewitched by narrow, untenable, and
uniquely modern assumptions about how beliefs and ideas develop
and interlock, then we can wrongly presume that "source" means
directly found in or deduced from Scripture. This assumption
makes Origen's claim seem absurd, for On First Principles is a
speculative treatise that is deeply indebted to Neoplatonism. Yet
if we drop these modern assumptions and instead see Origen's
grand theology of creation, time, embodiment, evil, redemption,
and consummation as a way of shaping a metaphysical horizon
that allows us to read the Bible biblically, then we can grasp the

19. See, for example, Peter Enns, *Inspiration and Incarnation: Evangelicals and
the Problem of the Old Testament* (Grand Rapids: Baker Academic, 2005), 17–21.
20. Origen, *On First Principles* 1.preface.1. Translation by G. W. Butterworth,
reprinted as Origen, *On First Principles* (Gloucester, MA: Peter Smith, 1973).

true meaning of his claim. "Think of reality this way," Origen should be read as saying, "and you will be able to enter more fully into the wisdom of the Scriptures, because you will be thinking scripturally." Origen's system is unique, and in many respects defective. But in my estimation, his ambitious effort to "scripturalize" metaphysics characterizes the Nicene tradition as a whole.[21]

The Nicene tradition is complex and unruly. I am a theological traditionalist, which means I presume this tradition to be sound. When it seems wrong, I'm probably guilty of misunderstanding what it teaches. But it is quite possible to have a less trusting disposition. The presumption of accordance allows one to regard the Nicene tradition as in need of correction by the interpretation of Scripture. This corrective impulse was not unique to the Reformers of the sixteenth century. The Nicene tradition as a whole should be understood as an argument (often heated) about how best to account for the truth of *everything* in light of scriptural teaching, church practice, and proclamation—an argument that extends across many generations. Like all large-scale, ongoing, and communally conducted arguments, it features constant restatements, reconsiderations, and revisions. But even for those who emphasize ongoing reformation, there are many steady and constant points of consensus in the Nicene tradition. And as a scripturally informed economy of truth, it remains peerless. I defy anyone to identify a way of thinking about God, history, and human destiny that is at once more metaphysically self-conscious than the Nicene tradition and more thoroughly and constantly invested with exegetical substance.[22]

21. For a winsome and sympathetic description of Origen's systematic project, see Rowan Williams, "Origen," in *The First Theologians*, ed. G. R. Evans (Oxford: Blackwell, 2003). For an effort to show the exegetical genius of Origen's theology, see chapter 3 below.

22. On the close connection between doctrine and exegesis in the early development of the Nicene tradition, see R. R. Reno and John J. O'Keefe, *Sanctified Vision: An Introduction to Early Christian Interpretation of the Bible* (Baltimore: Johns Hopkins University Press, 2005).

My own efforts to write biblical commentary have made me
acutely aware of the conceptual rigor and interpretive power found
in the Nicene tradition. When I grappled with the puzzle of the
traditional view of God and creation in relation to the first verses
of Genesis, I came to be impressed by the exegetical roots of the
doctrine of creation out of nothing. As a metaphysical claim about
God and reality, the classical doctrine has no basis in common
sense or ancient science. (One problem with Origen's *On First
Principles* is that he tried to preserve the cosmology of Neoplatonism, which he believed was the best science of his day.) *Creatio
ex nihilo* emerges instead out of sustained attempts to formulate
the ontological parsimony implied in the Old Testament polemic
against idolatry. In the history of theology, the doctrine of creation
out of nothing provided an important background assumption
for discussions of divine presence and action within history, most
importantly in the person of Jesus Christ.[23] Without a metaphysical horizon informed by *creatio ex nihilo*, reading the Bible as a
coherent narrative about the God of Israel who raised Jesus from
the dead is very difficult.

If we keep in mind the exegetical sources and pressures that
spurred the development of Nicene doctrine, we can grasp the
historical rationale for theological exegesis. When we use doctrine
to orient ourselves, to frame our exegetical questions, and to draw
out the significance of a biblical passage—when we are engaging
in the multifaceted enterprise that I have been calling theological
exegesis—we draw on intellectual resources that have been developed and refined for the specific purpose of thinking biblically
about the Bible. The presumption of accordance between how we
read the Bible and how we understand church teaching is primitive to the Christian tradition. There never has been a moment in
the history of Christianity when exegesis and doctrine have not

23. See especially Irenaeus, *Against Heresies* 1. The doctrine of creation provides
the main backdrop for Irenaeus's criticisms of the cogency of Gnostic soteriology,
as well as the basis for his own theology of the incarnation.

been intertwined in a complex but integrated intellectual practice. Never, that is, until the modern era.

———

For all sorts of complex reasons, contemporary biblical scholars are troubled by theological exegesis. Needless to say, scholars without Christian commitments do not entertain the notion that church doctrines state important truths about God, or anything else for that matter. For them, the arguments I have presented for theological exegesis can seem like only pseudo-sophisticated expressions of religious fundamentalism. Yet even biblical scholars who are believers remain uneasy about theological exegesis. They fear that more will be lost than gained by the introduction of doctrinal concerns into the practice of interpretation. And what do they fear will be lost? Having listened to and read the concerns of men and women of faith who are committed to modern historical-critical study, I find myself identifying two kinds of worries. The first is institutional and political; the second is textual and theological.

In *The Bible after Babel: Historical Criticism in a Postmodern Age*, John Collins defines modern biblical study in a new way. Our present postmodern skepticism has undermined confidence that historical-critical procedures can deliver conclusive answers to questions about what various biblical texts once meant for their original writers, editors, and readers. Nevertheless, as Collins notes, the rules for historical study remain normative, for they are academic rather than confessional, based on modern canons of historical analysis, not classical principles of faith. The shift away from doctrine has allowed for free and open discussion. Collins observes that historical criticism "has created an arena where people of different faith commitments can work together and have meaningful conversations."[24] A Jew, a Christian, and

24. John J. Collins, *The Bible after Babel: Historical Criticism in a Postmodern Age* (Grand Rapids: Eerdmans, 2005), 10. For an excellent discussion of Collins and the shift toward a political justification for historical-critical method, see Michael C.

an atheist can agree about what counts as a good argument for determining the sources for the J writer, for example, or the *Sitz im Leben* of imprecatory psalms. This agreement creates a neutral institutional space for biblical study, allowing for conversation across confessional divides.

Collins is right. The range of conversations about the Bible made possible by modern critical methods has been of great value. Not only has this method built a culture of cooperation and mutual learning among scholars from different backgrounds; it has also injected fresh insights into old theological debates. The new consensus about Paul developed in recent decades played a decisive role in overcoming confessional divides in the Lutheran and Roman Catholic traditions, an ecumenical breakthrough that was given clear expression in the *Joint Declaration on the Doctrine of Justification*, which was put forward in the late 1990s.[25] I can imagine a different but equally significant consensus emerging about biblical ideas of covenant and Christian supersessionism as Jewish scholars participate in New Testament study.

Contemporary biblical scholars should persevere in their inquiries, just as Christian scholars should carry forward their work in psychology, physics, and other disciplines that play roles in Christian self-understanding. The virtue of faith invites us to engage in a remarkable range of intellectual projects and conversations. There is no reason why modern historical study and other methods should not play an ongoing role in the church's reading of the Bible.

However, Collins makes the unwarranted assumption that modern biblical study is intrinsically antithetical to theological exegesis, when, in fact, only the historical-critical claim to final interpretive authority contradicts a theological approach. Reviews

---

Legaspi, "What Ever Happened to Historical Criticism?," *Journal of Religion & Society* 9 (2007).

25. I discuss the contribution of biblical scholarship to this ecumenical agreement in "The Joint Declaration on the Doctrine of Justification: An Outsider's View," *Pro Ecclesia* 7, no. 4 (1998): 427–48.

of some of the early volumes in the Brazos Theological Commentary on the Bible exemplify this false assumption. In many cases, reviewers trained as modern biblical scholars have objected to what they regard as spurious typologies and unwarranted intrusions of christological claims, as well as a general tendency to move from the biblical text to theological analysis. Rather than entering into these modes of analysis to offer criticisms of their cogency, biblical scholars have tended to resort to academic policing, unconsciously making the false inference that because the historical-critical method would not lead one to say x about the book of Jonah or the Gospel of Matthew, therefore x should not be said.

The rationales I have given for theological exegesis directly challenge the supreme interpretive authority many accord to modern biblical criticism. This challenge cannot be avoided. Unless one rejects nearly all forms of classical ecclesiology—Protestant, Catholic, and Orthodox—any effort by a Christian to explain what the Bible fully and finally says will need to account for the teachings of the church. Moreover, given how deeply the Nicene tradition has been influenced by biblical interpretation during its centuries of development, anyone who seeks a biblically shaped horizon for interpretation will need to reckon with classical doctrine. In this instance, as in others, theology remains the queen of the sciences. Historical study of the Bible has a legitimate and perhaps necessary role in our contemporary context. But it cannot be sufficient for Christian readers, because its methods operate at a studied distance from what men and women of faith implicitly (Protestant) or explicitly (Catholic) regard as the most reliable guide to the truths of Scripture—church doctrine.

The second worry concerns the Bible in its particularity. Modern historical study often promotes close attention to textual detail. It naturally rebels against the way in which the metaphysical horizon of the Nicene tradition can encourage theological readers to develop lines of analysis that run toward conceptual questions rather than textual ones. For example, my reading of the first verses of Genesis moves very quickly from what the text says to an analysis of what is entailed in the doctrine of creation out of nothing. I would not be surprised if contemporary biblical scholars note this shift with dismay. The worries intensify with christological readings of the Old Testament. Biblical scholars are concerned that this approach bounces from the Old to the New Testament and back again without regard for the vast differences of cultural and historical context. Even a decision to use the final form of the canonical text can rankle, because it seems to ignore the multilayered reality of tradition and redaction that gives rise to the Bible as we have it today.

These worries about the loss of textual particularity and historical depth have theological legitimacy. The Bible does not speak to us in pithy doctrines. It is not a catechism thrown into narrative, poetic, or legal form. On the contrary, the Bible is thickly forested with history and culture. It confronts us with endless nuances of language and expression. Biblical scholars rightly regard their training as a sustained immersion in the endlessly multifaceted and plural worlds of the Bible. We fail to read fully and deeply, argues the modern biblical scholar, if we fail to enter into the almost trackless but beautiful wilderness of the Bible.

Here I find myself in full sympathy, but I must make some cautionary remarks. To begin, it is not the case that modern biblical study refrains from abstractions and always remains intimately engaged with the biblical text. Efforts to reconstruct the original context for the book of Exodus or the Gospel of John amount to elaborate speculative enterprises that rely on a raft of sociological, psychological, and historical assumptions. Redaction criticism can be used to dismember books of the Bible. One often finds modern scholars using this technique to explain away rather than interpret passages.[26] In practice, the modern genre of historical-critical

26. For a particularly egregious example, see Gerhard von Rad's explanation of why one can ignore Gen. 38: *Genesis: A Commentary*, trans. John H. Marks (Philadelphia: Westminster, 1972), 356–57.

commentary easily becomes an ossified template. Many historical-critical commentaries read like summaries of recent scholarship rather than fresh engagements with the biblical text.

Troublesome as those tendencies may be for those who cherish biblical particularity, there is a still greater danger. Modern biblical scholarship cannot sustain intellectual justification for its intensive focus on the canonical text. As the present evolution of graduate programs indicates, the natural subject matter for those who cleave to modern methods should not be the Old and New Testaments but rather ancient Near Eastern and Greco-Roman culture and religion. I do not object to this evolution. It strikes me as the proper avenue of development if one wishes to pursue a purely historical approach to ancient texts, and I predict it will lead to exciting new insights. But we need to refrain from illusions. This trend will not encourage the development of the deep immersion in Scripture that many wrongly imagine is intrinsic to the modern historical-critical tradition.

Theological exegesis does not approach the Bible with predetermined interpretations that glide smoothly over the surfaces of the Bible. The contrary should be the case. Because theological exegesis presumes that church and Bible are on the same page, so to speak, the effect is to encourage rather than short-circuit concern for nuance, detail, and textual particularity. Given the presumption of accordance, judgments about how to read the Bible must invariably influence the ways in which we interpret doctrine. And conversely, our always-ongoing efforts to understand the Nicene tradition should leaven our always-incomplete interpretations of the Bible. The overall effect, it seems to me, will be neither wooden applications of doctrine to exegesis nor a systematic neglect of the organic diversity of the Bible. The rationale I have given for theological exegesis challenges rather than encourages complacency, as I hope the exegetical material provided in this volume convincingly demonstrates. Accordance must be presumed by the faithful Christian, to be sure. But to presume is not to see and explain. Accordance often needs to be discerned with considerable effort. One must enter more deeply into both doctrine and Scripture in order to find one's way toward the truth of Christ to which they both testify.

In the end, the goal of exegesis is always to bear witness to the truth that the text reveals. Only intellectual ideologues write commentaries devoted to the advancement of labels and methods. Like Origen and Bernard of Clairvaux, Luther and Karl Barth, Rudolf Bultmann and Gerhard von Rad—and like graduate students writing postcolonial interpretations of Joshua and Judges—interpreters of the Bible want to bring out the truth in the Bible, the truth suggested by, signified in, and derived from the Bible. Take your pick of metaphors and prepositions and their implied epistemological assumptions: interpreters may oppose the Christian tradition or they may endorse it, but they are always aiming to see what the Bible reveals, whether conceived in terms of historical development, power relations, or salvation in Christ.

Neither the common ambition to "see" the truth in the Bible nor the often divergent, even contradictory, readings of so many different interpreters who approach the Bible in so many different ways should surprise us. Truth is what we seek when we engage our minds. And what is on our minds shapes what we see. To be a Christian is to believe that the truth found in the Bible is the same truth we enter into by way of baptism, the same truth we confess in our creeds, the same truth we receive in the bread and wine of the Eucharist. Theological exegesis, therefore, is not a method. It is simply an approach that does not ignore the truth taught from pulpits and conveyed in confessions when embarking on the difficult task of trying to discern the truth that the Bible reveals.

2

THEOLOGY AND INTERPRETATION

WHEN THE CORE GROUP that would become the Scripture Project gathered for the first time in the late 1990s, they came to a consensus. As co-leader Ellen Davis reported: "The most fundamental need," the group agreed, is "to learn again to read and teach the Bible confessionally within mainstream North American and European Christianity."[1] It is a convincing judgment, one that remains widely shared by those concerned about the future of Christianity in the West. For too long, theology—understood as the knowledge of and skill in analyzing, defending, and applying the doctrines of the church—has not interacted in meaningful ways with modern interpretations of the Bible. The way in which we read and teach the Bible does not inform the way in which we teach our faith and govern our lives.

Old Testament scholar Walter Moberly thinks that modern biblical study has given rise to a "curious situation." He notes, "To be Christian means, at least in part, the acceptance and appropriation of certain theological doctrines and patterns of living." This is the side of church teaching that we presume to be

---

1. Ellen F. Davis, "Teaching the Bible Confessionally in the Church," in *The Art of Reading Scripture*, ed. Ellen F. Davis and Richard B. Hays (Grand Rapids: Eerdmans, 2003), 9.

in accord with Scripture. "Yet the task of reading the Bible 'critically' has regularly been defined precisely in terms of the exclusion
of these doctrines and patterns of living from the interpretive
process."[2] Decades ago, Van Harvey observed, "Anyone teaching
the origins of Christianity to college undergraduates or divinity
students cannot help but be struck by the enormous gap between
what the average layperson believes to be historically true about
Jesus of Nazareth and what a great majority of New Testament
scholars have concluded."[3] Whether you put your hope in renewed
influence of doctrine or revision of church teaching guided by
modern biblical scholarship, the situation is the same. Instead of
accordance, we find discord. It is hard to imagine a more fundamental crisis.[4]

"Theological exegesis" describes the mode of reading that
we hope can overcome the alienation of theologically informed
"church talk" from the kind of "Bible talk" encouraged by close
readings of Scripture. But the concept of theological exegesis often
remains opaque. We too often think of theological interpretation as something distinct from textually grounded analysis. In

2. R. W. L. Moberly, *The Bible, Theology, and Faith: A Study of Abraham and
Jesus* (Cambridge: Cambridge University Press, 2000), 5.

3. Van Harvey, "New Testament Scholarship and Christian Belief," in *Jesus in
History and Myth*, ed. R. Joseph Hoffman and Gerald A. Larue (Buffalo: Prometheus,
1986), 193.

4. One of the most important twentieth-century Protestant theological moves has
been to interpret this crisis as a positive development. By this account, the genius
of the Reformation was the shattering of all works of the law by the doctrine of
justification. The modern application of historical-critical principles to doctrine and
Scripture completes the Reformer's project. Historical-critical method undermines
these authorities, clearing the way for a true and pure Protestant atmosphere of
faith entirely free from temptation to rest in external forms of assurance, including
creed and Scripture. For a classic statement of this argument, see Gerhard Ebeling,
"The Significance of the Critical Historical Method for Church and Theology in
Protestantism," first published in 1950 and reprinted in revised form in *Word and
Faith* (London: SCM, 1963), 17–61. For a broader statement of the same argument,
see Paul Tillich's characterizations of the Protestant Principle in *The Protestant Era*
(Chicago: University of Chicago Press, 1948). For an illustration of the consequent
mentality, see John Shelby Spong, *Rescuing the Bible from Fundamentalism* (San
Francisco: HarperSanFrancisco, 1992).

the preface to the Interpretation series, one of the most widely consulted commentary series in the second half of the twentieth century, the editors tell us that exegesis involves two different mental operations. Good exegetes are "to deal with what the texts say and to discern their meaning for faith and life."[5] In this double task, Krister Stendahl's influential distinction between "what it meant for them" and "what it means for us" continues to echo.[6]

The problem is that the church acknowledges no such distinction. Christian readers have always recognized that certain texts require grammatical clarification. The early church fathers saw that in some instances good exposition demands consideration of historical contexts. At times, doctrine is explicitly brought to bear. At other times, moral conclusions are drawn and contemporary applications are made. And for premodern readers, this diversity of focus and concern functioned within a single interpretive enterprise. They did not seek a "theological meaning" distinct from the text's "historical meaning." Instead, the church distinguished between good and bad exegesis. Only modernist ideologies of meaning and history sustain thoroughgoing distinctions between theological exegesis and other modes of interpretation.

With the witness of the older tradition in mind, I want to take another stab at describing the kind of interpretation sought by those who wish to reunite confessional teaching with good exegesis. Using the term from the previous chapter, my aim is to outline what "good reading" looks like when we seek to discern the accordance of doctrine and Scripture. And I want to pursue this account of "good interpretation" without relying on contrasts between "theological" readings, on the one hand, and the historical-critical methods developed in recent centuries, on the other.

5. James Luther Mays, Patrick D. Miller, and Paul J. Achtemeier, "Series Preface," in Ralph P. Martin, *Ephesians, Colossians, and Philemon*, Interpretation: A Bible Commentary for Preaching and Teaching (Louisville: Westminster John Knox, 1991), v.

6. Krister Stendahl, "Biblical Theology, Contemporary," *The Interpreter's Dictionary of the Bible*, vol. 1, *A–D* (Nashville: Abingdon, 1962), 418–32.

I'll start with a recapitulation of the relationship between doctrine (by which I mean not only official teachings but also the church's liturgical practice, moral formation, and spiritual discipline—what Moberly calls "patterns of living") and Scripture. I'll then turn to one of my own efforts to read "theologically." In conclusion, I'll offer programmatic remarks about modern historical-critical study and its relation to the good interpretation we ought to seek as faithful readers of Scripture.

What follows repeats themes developed in the previous chapter. In my estimation, this is necessary. As I mentioned earlier, we're so deeply imbued with dreams of identifying the right "method" that we have a hard time accepting the straightforward logic of theological interpretation, which creates expectations and puts demands on readers but does not issue in a set pattern for or formal criteria of good interpretation.

In the aftermath of the Reformation, interpretation of the Bible was hotly contested, and the relationship between doctrine and Scripture itself became a matter of theological controversy. Yet, as I outlined in the previous chapter, a consensus undergirded debates between Protestants and Catholics. Everyone presumed that doctrine must accord with Scripture. For most of the post-Reformation period, the Catholic Church insisted upon an almost complete correspondence between Roman teaching and Scripture properly interpreted, allowing only for the possibility that biblical exegesis, like doctrine, can develop toward fuller and fuller exposition of already recognized truths.[7] The Protestant tradition's interest in ongoing reform of the church made the relationship between doctrine and Scripture less tightly defined,

7. This was in some measure modified at Vatican II. See "Dogmatic Constitution on Divine Revelation," *Dei Verbum* (The Holy See: Web Archive), sec. 22, https://www.vatican.va/archive/hist_councils/ii_vatican_council/documents/vat-ii_const_19651118_dei-verbum_en.html.

but the underlying logic was similar. What the Bible says and what the church teaches may not be in full accord at present, but they should be, and the goal of both exegesis and theology is to maximize this correspondence.

This is not a book about ecumenical theology, so I cannot address the differences between Catholic, Lutheran, and Reformed views on the link between doctrine and biblical interpretation, a difference that turns on how our traditions define the church's teaching authority. But I hope that by now readers will allow that Protestants and Catholics agree on the accordance of doctrine with Scripture. How could it be otherwise? The Bible is the Word of God. The church is the body of Christ. If we affirm these two truth claims, we will end up insisting that what is taught by the church substantially accords with what the Bible says (and that if it doesn't, it should!). Thus, as I argued in the first chapter, however bitterly we may debate church authority, confessional documents, theories of inerrancy, and particular interpretations, the presumption of accordance is not itself controversial.

With this close relationship between church doctrine and the content of the Bible in mind, we can return to our current crisis of church-formed faith detached from biblical interpretation and think more clearly. The problem is not that something labeled "theology" has not adequately engaged something else called "biblical studies." We do not want for interdisciplinary study. Instead, we are facing a crisis within our churches. We hold that the doctrine of the Trinity is a foundational dogma—and we are told that it is not to be found in the Bible. We believe that Jesus Christ is the Messiah who fulfills the law and the prophets—and we are instructed that reading the Old Testament in light of the New commits the sin of anachronism. I could go on with more examples, but we all know the scandal: what the churches teach and what many biblical scholars tell us the Bible means often seem at odds. In view of this fundamental and

debilitating problem, let us entertain a minimal (but significant)
definition of theological exegesis. It is *any* reading that moves
in the opposite direction. Interpretation is "theological" insofar as it shows how church teaching accords with what the Bible
says.

At this point some readers are no doubt squirming. Is the purpose of exegesis to prove doctrine, as if doctrine were the great
vehicle of divine truth and not the Scriptures themselves? The challenge is justified. In both the Protestant and Catholic traditions,
there has been a tendency to see doctrine as the purified, reasoned,
and fully clarified "content" of Scripture. In a late nineteenth-
century dogmatic textbook, *A Manual of Catholic Theology*,
the authors describe doctrine as "materially complete," "formally
perfect," and capable of universal application. This textbook goes
on to contrast these luminous qualities to Scripture's lack of "systematic arrangement," which makes the Bible often obscure and
"exposed to many false interpretations." The historical character
of Scripture means that its great truths are "expressed in the metaphorical language of the East." As a result, Scripture is "unfit for
the general use of people."[8] If we would but learn our Baltimore
Catechism, then we would be fully and reliably formed in God's
truth!

I call this sentiment "doctrinal supersessionism," which I define
as the functional replacement of Scripture by doctrine as the living font of our faith. There is nothing uniquely Roman about this
supersession of Scripture by doctrine. In his influential work of
Protestant systematic theology, Friedrich Schleiermacher makes
the observation that Catholics and Protestants share the same
Bible. For this reason, Scripture cannot be authoritative for Protestants (or Catholics), since it cannot provide the authoritative
teaching that shows why Protestantism is true while Catholicism
is defective. This leads Schleiermacher to elevate church doctrine

8. Joseph Wilhelm and Thomas Scannell, *A Manual of Catholic Theology* (London: Kegan Paul, Trench, Trübner, 1890), 59.

over the Bible. "The confessional documents of the Evangelical Church, collectively, are, as it were, given a prior place to the New Testament Scriptures themselves."[9] The irony is palpable. The doctrine of *sola scriptura* becomes more important than what is said in Scripture!

This supersession of Scripture by doctrine needs to be resisted.[10] Although doctrines certainly teach truths about God, they do not reveal God. Influenced by powerful criticisms of defective modes of Christian formation that are encouraged by the view that doctrine is superior to Scripture, the Second Vatican Council gave urgent and eloquent voice to the need for a renewal of faith deeply informed by the Bible. It is not the case that the church draws truths out of Scripture, encodes them into doctrines, and then moves on.[11] As Vatican II teaches, the church never ceases to receive "the bread of life from the table both of God's word and of Christ's body," and "therefore, like the Christian religion itself, all the preaching of the Church must be nourished and regulated by Sacred Scripture."[12] No matter how correct doctrine might be in a formal sense, the urgent task of bringing the biblical word to bear upon the life of the church is ongoing. "The force and power in the word of God is so great," teaches the council, "that it stands as the support and energy of the Church, the strength of

9. Friedrich Schleiermacher, *The Christian Faith*, trans. H. R. Mackintosh and J. S. Stewart (Edinburgh: T&T Clark, 1928), 112.

10. For a full account of why Western Christianity has tended toward doctrinal supersessionism, see R. R. Reno, "Theology in the Ruins of the Church," *Pro Ecclesia* 12, no. 1 (2003): 15–36.

11. As Joseph Ratzinger observes in his commentary on *Dei Verbum*, the Second Vatican Council's "Dogmatic Constitution on Divine Revelation," the history of discussion at the council suggests that "there was a gradual reduction of the idea of progress." Ratzinger registers his own view that "from an ecumenical point of view, the only sensible thing is to give up the idea of progress" (*Commentary on the Documents of Vatican II*, ed. Herbert Vorgrimler [New York: Herder & Herder, 1969], 3:266). The primary dynamic of Catholic doctrinal development has been one of return and renewal. Doctrine does not advance beyond Scripture; instead, doctrine brings the church back to Scripture.

12. Vatican II, "Dogmatic Constitution on Divine Revelation," *Dei Verbum*, sec. 21.

faith for her sons, the food of the soul, the pure and everlasting source of spiritual life."[13]

Whether informed by Protestant confessions or Catholic doctrine, church teaching must be infused by the apostolic vitality of Scripture. This is done through theological interpretation, which seeks to discern how church teaching accords with what the Bible says. In seeking this accordance, theological exegesis renews the language of faith. It re-saturates the life of the church with what the Bible says. Let's put the matter in a formula: the more readily a reading of the Bible enters into and reinvigorates the life and practice of the church, the more fully "theological" is our scriptural interpretation.

With these brief reflections, I have restated the account of theological exegesis developed in the previous chapter, although in somewhat different terms. This may dissatisfy some. My approach can seem like verbal hand-waving—interpretation is "theological" if it brings doctrine and Scripture into accordance. We are so accustomed to thinking in terms of methods and techniques rather than ends and goals that this definition of theological exegesis appears to be an illusion of logic rather than a real possibility for Christian readers of the Bible. The hoary distinction between what the Bible *meant* and what it *means*, between reading the text "critically and responsibly" and reading it "naively and piously," retains a powerful grip. We worry that without a distinct and superordinate role for historical-critical reading, our exegesis will lack credibility and discipline.

Instead of responding theoretically, I want to return to my remarks on *creatio ex nihilo* in the previous chapter (developed more extensively in chapter 5). I apologize for rehearsing this material. But I have found it of great value to illustrate "theological exegesis" rather than to digress into theoretical explanations. If we work with doctrine and the Bible together, we can see that

---

13. Vatican II, "Dogmatic Constitution on Divine Revelation," *Dei Verbum*, sec. 21.

they illuminate each other, and the tendentious contrast between "objective exegesis" and "pious reading" loses its power.

———

Consider the first verses of Genesis. Here we find biblical material both ambiguous and fraught. The Hebrew admits of different senses. Should we read the first verse as "In the beginning God created," conveying the sense that we are at the absolute beginning? Or should we read this opening verse in a more modest way? Modern scholars propose a new translation: "In the beginning, when God created." This suggests a more limited notion of creation. And what are we to make of the next verse and its mention of the unformed earth and the darkness and the face of the waters? Did God make the heavens and earth out of a preexisting primal substance?

In his *Unfinished Literal Commentary on Genesis*, Augustine raises these questions and offers a variety of interpretive suggestions. He makes the reasonable observation that the Bible does not provide every detail. Therefore, we can suppose that in the first moment God creates all the elements mentioned in Genesis 1:2—the formless earth, the darkness, the water, and so forth. It is evident to us that loyalty to church doctrine is guiding Augustine at this point. He admits as much, saying, "Whichever of these opinions is true, we must believe that God is the Maker and Creator of all things."[14] To recall the account of theological exegesis detailed in the previous chapter, Augustine reads so as to ensure that doctrine accords with Scripture. *Creatio ex nihilo*, creation out of nothing, is normative doctrine, and Augustine brings his reading into conformity with it.

As modern men and women, we are urged to step back and say, "Yes, of course, Augustine accepted the authority of doctrine, and

14. Augustine, *Unfinished Literal Commentary on Genesis* 4, in *On Genesis*, trans. Edmund Hill, The Works of Saint Augustine I/13 (Hyde Park, NY: New City, 2002).

look what happened. He was indifferent to what the Bible really says." The plain sense of the second verse of Genesis suggests that there was something upon which God acted in creation. The modern historical-critical mode of analysis adds credence to the plain sense of this verse, pointing to the many combat myths of creation from ancient literature that might have influenced the ancient Israelite worldview. Furthermore, scholars have pointed out that the Old Testament itself often pictures the origins of the world in the same fashion. Aside from 2 Maccabees 7:28, the declarations of God's creative sovereignty and power throughout the Bible do not specify creation out of nothing. And so it would seem that Augustine's deference to the doctrine of *creatio ex nihilo* presents a classic case of preconceived theological ideas subverting the text. A rigid system of doctrine is being imposed upon Scripture, silencing Scripture's own voice. It is one thing to accept responsibility for showing the concordance of Scripture and doctrine, we insist; but we must be sure not to lose the text in the process!

These were among the concerns that led to the formulation of a dogma of modern biblical study: doctrine must be excluded from exegesis. As Benjamin Jowett wrote in the nineteenth century, the role of the interpreter is to recover "the simple words" of Scripture. This requires the reader to "clear away the remains of dogmas, systems, controversies" that tempt us to misread. By returning to the text in its purity, Jowett promises, we will commune with the minds of the original authors. Scriptures once smothered by doctrine will return to life.[15]

Unfortunately, the results of applying this modern dogma have been otherwise. Insofar as our churches continue to recite the Nicene Creed, any reading of the opening material in Genesis that fails to conclude that the text is compatible with the doctrine of

---

15. See Benjamin Jowett, "On the Interpretation of Scripture," in *Essays and Reviews* (London: Parker, 1860), 338–39.

creatio ex nihilo removes these verses from the functional piety of believers and weakens the role of the Bible in the life of the church. How can one affirm the doctrine that God creates out of nothing and at the same time agree that the Bible teaches otherwise without sidelining Scripture? We often try to put a Band-Aid on the wound by adopting a fuzzy and emotive view of doctrine, allowing us to avoid confronting the contradiction. Whatever our tactics, the upshot is the same. Doctrine becomes less scriptural and our biblical literacy less doctrinal. This happens whenever a biblical interpreter concludes that the Bible says something other than what the church teaches. Instead of coming to life, the voice of Scripture is muffled, even silenced, in the life of the church. This is why the biblical scholars who participated in the Scripture Project were eager to recover "confessional" readings. They sensed that discerning accordance between doctrine and Scripture is essential if we are to revive scriptural literacy among the faithful.

We do not need to choose between loyalty to doctrine and attentiveness to the textual particularity of Scripture. That's because classical doctrine is not *sui generis*. Dogmas such as *creatio ex nihilo* guide an overall reading of Scripture that brings Scripture to life rather than stifling its voice. For this reason, there is nothing "complacent" about accepting the authority of doctrine in the work of exegesis. On the contrary, the *difficulty* of bringing Scripture and doctrine into some kind of intellectually and spiritually satisfactory relationship infuses exegesis with urgency, energy, and creativity.

Creatio ex nihilo is not a free-floating doctrine. It arises from a complex set of exegetical judgments that operate across the entire biblical text. As I noted in chapter 1, the Old Testament campaign against idolatry has a recurring structure. Idols are not weak, ineffective, or inadequate; they are empty and lifeless. The New Testament carries forward the same view of idols as lifeless and powerless.

In many instances in Scripture, warnings against the danger of lifeless idols are made against the background of larger affirmations of God's creative sovereignty. Because God creates out of nothing, there is nothing (*nihil*) other than the one true God and all the things he has made. Thus, idolatry is not a simple mistake or miscalculation. It is not a misplaced loyalty to a semi-divine or primeval power unable to measure up to the power and glory of the Lord Almighty. Idolatry is loyalty to *nihil*, a devotion to lifelessness, which is why the Old Testament often portrays idolatry as the worst of sins. Idol worship encourages and reflects a desire for nothingness, a choice of death that Moses warns against repeatedly in Deuteronomy. Saint Paul's account of sin begins with a primordial turn from the living God—whose creative glory is readily "seen through the things he has made" (Rom. 1:20)—and toward "images" (1:20–23). This genealogy of sin reiterates the judgments of the Old Testament. There is no place to stand between God and creation—and to try to do so only results in an irrational, self-defeating loyalty to nothingness. Not surprisingly, therefore, the themes of idolatry and loyalty set the stage for the explicit affirmation of *creatio ex nihilo* in 2 Maccabees 7:28.

The apparent conflict between two biblical claims about God provides another reason to read Genesis 1 under the control of the doctrine of *creatio ex nihilo*. On the one hand, many passages describe God as wholly other. He is the transcendent deity who cannot be framed within the finite world. On the other hand, God is a character within the biblical story. He commands and speaks. So, which shall it be? Is God without or within? Is God wholly other or does he operate within the unfolding drama of salvation history? The contrastive choice between universality and particularity is all the more dramatic in classical Christology. Divine transcendence seems utterly inconsistent with incarnation: foolishness to the Greeks.

In the previous chapter, I pointed out the ontological parsimony of *creatio ex nihilo*. This helps us resolve the apparent contradiction between the transcendence and the presence of God. The doctrine of creation out of nothing teaches that there is nothing prior to creation, which means that there is nothing for God not to be. This parsimony is evident in the famous declaration of God's name (Exod. 3:14): God is who he is simply because he is who he is. God is not God because he is not something else.

Because *creatio ex nihilo* formulates God's transcendence in terms of uniqueness rather than by appeal to his supremacy or priority over primal matter, the transcendence of God is consistent with his immediacy and presence to finite reality. God leaves nothing behind in his presence in history; he betrays or contradicts nothing "divine" by drawing near. A biblical reader need not choose between the universal God and the Lord who acts in space and time. Nor need the reader parse divinity and humanity in the unified person of Jesus Christ.[16] By contrast, a reading of Genesis 1:2 that contradicts *creatio ex nihilo* and its implied ontological parsimony undermines the capacity of scriptural readers to interpret the God of Israel as the universal deity. Worse still, it makes the New Testament's witness to God incarnate incoherent.

Here we get a glimpse of the fruitful role of doctrine in exegesis. *Creatio ex nihilo* guides us toward a reading of some ambiguous words and phrases in Genesis 1:2 that allows us to sustain very straightforward readings of countless other biblical verses. How, then, could a rejection of this doctrine, supposedly for the sake of preserving the integrity of the biblical text, succeed on its own terms? If we set aside *creatio ex nihilo*, we cannot affirm the plain sense of the many biblical verses that speak of God's presence. Classical doctrine was developed precisely to avoid this problem.

Finally, a reading of the first chapter of Genesis governed by the doctrine of creation out of nothing underwrites the christological

---

16. See Origen, *Contra Celsum* 4.5. For a helpful discussion of the way in which *creatio ex nihilo* provides crucial background for christological doctrine, see Robert Sokolowski, *The God of Faith and Reason: Foundations of Christian Theology* (Washington, DC: Catholic University of America Press, 1995), 31–40.

maximalism that characterizes classical Christian interpretation of Scripture.[17] Irenaeus based his rejection of Gnostic accounts of Jesus on a complex refutation of the Gnostic doctrine of creation.[18] Gnostic teaching presumed that this world is the final stage of a cosmic evolution characterized by many layers of spiritual or supernatural reality emanating from the one transcendent and eternal deity. With a richly populated ontological scheme at their disposal, Gnostic teachers were able to avoid what they took to be the metaphysical absurdity of saying that Jesus is God incarnate. They could assign to Jesus an intermediate redemptive role. He is above us in ontological significance, pulling us up to the next higher link in the Great Chain of Being.

Irenaeus's arguments against the Gnostics underline the importance of the doctrine of creation out of nothing. That doctrine's rigorous exclusion of any preexisting substance other than God himself means that either Jesus must be simply a man or he is God incarnate. There are no other ontological alternatives. This is not a narrowly christological matter. It has to do with the larger *sola gratia* structure of so much of the Bible. Saint Paul's analysis of Abraham's justification, and by extension the larger project of divine blessing, emphasizes the lack of mediating realities between God and finite reality. Upon what might Abraham rely other than God, "who gives life to the dead and calls into existence the things that do not exist" (Rom. 4:17)? All other powers are "as good as dead" (Rom. 4:19), and thus "no one might boast in the presence of God" (1 Cor. 1:29). The ontological parsimony entailed by *creatio ex nihilo* eliminates half measures, and, as Paul reasons, we are forced to rely on God alone as the power of salvation. Paul's arguments for a *sola gratia* account of salvation,

17. For the use of the term "christological maximalism" and suggestions about its importance in the early Christian project of forming a coherent overall interpretation of the data of Scripture and tradition, see George A. Lindbeck, *The Nature of Doctrine: Religion and Theology in a Postliberal Age* (Philadelphia: Westminster, 1984), 92–96.

18. Irenaeus, *Against Heresies* 1.

arguments central to the gospel, depend upon a reading of the opening of Genesis that accords with the doctrine of creation out of nothing.

My goal here has not been to provide an exhaustive account of how to read Genesis. I'll have much more to say on that in chapter 5. Instead, I have tried to illustrate a simple point about theological exegesis. Exercising ourselves to see the concord between Scripture and doctrine does not silence Scripture. Christian doctrine is a nearly two-thousand-year-long research project into the inner cogency of the Bible. The church's teachings were not developed as metaphysical speculations. They arose in order to bring to life in our minds the full sweep of Scripture. Therefore, if we read Scripture theologically—that is to say, if we read it in ways that show the concord between doctrine and Scripture—we will find our exegetical judgments both deepened and extended across the biblical text, the opposite of the "silencing" of Scripture warned against by those anxious to defend the authority of method.

———

Nothing I have said about the nature of theological interpretation contradicts the conviction that modern historical-critical study of the Bible remains a sophisticated and helpful mode of reading. Applying modern techniques of textual analysis can help us enter into the diversity and complexity of the biblical text. I remember reading one of Gerd Theissen's studies of the social setting of Paul's letters decades ago.[19] Having a vivid sense of the social context liberated me from my unconscious and stultifying assumption that Paul (and all of Scripture) uttered timeless truths into the great void of eternity. To hear Paul speak to real people in an actual community did not make him seem distant and diminished; it made Paul's voice living and present.

19. Gerd Theissen, *The Social Setting of Pauline Christianity: Essays on Corinth* (Philadelphia: Fortress, 1982).

Yet, for all that I have gained from historical-critical study of the Bible, I reject efforts to "build bridges" between theology and biblical studies. Theology is not fundamentally distinct from biblical interpretation. As I hope my brief discussion of Genesis and creation out of nothing illustrates, doctrine has exegetical origins and purposes. For this reason, doctrine can play a fruitful role in exegesis, not a sterile or destructive one, as so many modern critics have presumed.

Modern ways of reading have value. Historical study of ancient myths of creation and redaction criticism can help us see that the first chapter of Genesis is part of a priestly, legal, and temple-oriented strand running through the Pentateuch. Other modern historical-critical readings can also enrich and deepen our reading—as can literary, anthropological, and sociological ones. Frank Kermode's marvelous reading of the Gospel of Mark, *The Genesis of Secrecy*, strongly influenced me when I was an undergraduate in the early 1980s.[20] There is no reason to reject these techniques of analysis just because they operate without recourse to Christian assumptions about Scripture and doctrine. They often magnify and clarify our vision as readers.

But the crucial point is this: none of these methods can tell us what the Bible finally says. The analogy of scientific method helps clarify why this is the case. Scientists use experimental techniques to identify and clarify data. They can separate compounds into their constituent elements. They are able to carbon-date fossils, placing them in an accurate time line. But the redoubled application of these techniques will not produce a scientific theory. An electron microscope refines our sense of what the data are; its improved accuracy does not interpret that data. The same holds for historical-critical techniques. It is wrong to imagine that the intellectual methods that help us bring the Bible into focus as a diverse and historical document can also double as synthetic tools for interpretation.

20. Frank Kermode, *The Genesis of Secrecy: On the Interpretation of Narrative* (Cambridge, MA: Harvard University Press, 1979).

Modern attempts of alchemy that seek to transform sophisticated data analysis into a larger interpretive account are often far-fetched. They can be "allegorical" in the bad sense rejected by many in the Christian tradition. Reading Marcus Borg involves entering into occult theories of religious consciousness in which Paul Tillich is wedded to Norman O. Brown in the seventh epoch of the liberated ego as it bursts the bonds of social finitude. Even sober-minded Gerhard von Rad can sound as though he is conjuring concepts when he pronounces upon rather than reasons about theological topics in his commentary on Genesis. These unsatisfactory results are inevitable. Insofar as modern biblical studies self-consciously rejects classical Christian doctrines and takes up modern doctrines about religion and human consciousness (or the now-popular postmodern doctrines about society, power, and difference) and then uses these doctrines as the organizing principles for exegesis, we will get interpretations that make Scripture accord with sociology or sociological theories (or postmodern theories). Or we will get theological gestures that are vague and often untethered to the warp and woof of Scripture.

I do not want to end by pointing to the specks in the eyes of modern biblical scholars. There is a beam in my own theological eye. During the Second World War, Henri de Lubac wrote a series of lectures and essays. He wanted to understand why the Christian culture of Europe had failed to prevent the disaster of the continent-wide war, why "the whole edifice of European civilization seems to be collapsing." De Lubac had no illusions about the barbaric paganism of modern European ideologies. At this time he was working on a book that was published in 1945, *The Drama of Atheistic Humanism*. But in these essays he did not focus his attention on the enemy without. He was concerned about the rot within. As he observed, "At the root of everything, it must be said, there is a failure among Christians."[21]

21. Henri de Lubac, *Theology in History*, trans. Anne Englund Nash (San Francisco: Ignatius, 1996), 441.

According to de Lubac, the failure in his time—our failure today—had a number of sources. But the most important was and remains a loss of spiritual contact with the prime substance of Christian truth, Holy Scripture. Christians are without consequence in the present age, he writes, because of "the renunciation of knowing and using the Bible." This is especially true of the Old Testament. "Many theologians," he observes, "forgo acquiring a deeper knowledge of it, considering it an obscure domain, reserved for the exploration of a few, rare specialists."[22] This alienation from the Old Testament has remained all too true in our time. We—I do not exclude myself—neither see nor seek a living relationship between doctrine and Scripture. And if we do, our efforts are feeble.

Any Catholic theologian serious about the recovery of Scripture as the soul of theology must come to terms with the supersession of Scripture by doctrine that I noted in the manual tradition that dominated seminary education in the late nineteenth and early twentieth centuries. This legacy has by no means been overcome, in spite of Vatican II's exhortations to recover Scripture. Karl Rahner was the most influential Catholic theologian of the twentieth century. In his textbook *Foundations of Christian Faith*, he warns against "mere biblicism." According to Rahner, the old tradition of biblically informed theology is "basically obsolete." Modern historical-critical study has sole authority to determine the content of the Bible, he presumes, and intellectually respectable dogmatic theology "can make use of only as much scriptural data as is sufficiently certain from an honest exegete."[23] In Rahner's work, it turns out that very little "scriptural data" is useful. In the vast majority of his writings, all the cognitive energy goes into correlating post-Kantian "transcendental" philosophy with church doctrine, not doctrine with Scripture.

22. De Lubac, *Theology in History*, 226.
23. Karl Rahner, *Foundations of Christian Faith*, trans. William V. Dych (New York: Seabury, 1978), 14.

The preference for correlation to philosophy rather than concordance with Scripture is not only a Catholic vice. Modern Protestant theology has for too long functioned as a perverse theological scientism. "It is," writes John Webster, "fatally easy to prefer the relatively clean lines of doctrine to the much less manageable, untheorized material of the Bible."[24] It is tempting to dwell among the concepts of election and incarnation and perichoresis, as if they harbor a substantial, super-luminous truth within themselves. This approach fails to see that the purpose of doctrine and theology is to maximize the penetration of the mind into the world of Scripture. Nearly all theologians, Catholic and Protestant, are guilty of the neglect of Scripture that de Lubac bemoans. It is a spiritual vice we must address.[25]

The great doctrines of the church are exegetical judgments given communally authoritative form. They are living truths only insofar as we enter into them through the ongoing practice of biblical interpretation. Theology can digress into metaphysics and moral theory, into anthropology and any number of other topics. Theology is the queen of the sciences, and she has all things under her dominion. But the fundamental role of the queen is to discern God's truth by interpreting his revealed Word. The great variety of topics under the rubric of theology is for the sake of sustaining and extending its capacity to interpret the Bible. We must firmly reject the notion of "building a bridge" between something called theology and a supposedly very different enterprise called biblical scholarship. They should never be apart in the first place.

But there *is* a bridge that we need to build! What the church teaches and what the Bible says do not obviously accord with each other. The fit is never finalized, as the history of theological

24. John Webster, *Holy Scripture: A Dogmatic Sketch* (Cambridge: Cambridge University Press, 2003), 130.
25. On this imperative, see John Webster's exposition of the theological pedagogy of Zacharias Ursinus, with pointed contrasts to modern theological sensibilities (*Holy Scripture*, 107–35).

controversy and exegetical debate demonstrates. But on this point we should be clear-minded. The presumption that doctrine must accord with Scripture no more preempts questions or subverts clear thinking than the scientific conviction that theory must be related to data ends investigation or weakens reason. Knowing the ends or goals of inquiry energizes and sharpens rather than enervates and dulls. The presumption of accordance forces us to see and explain how church teaching accords with Scripture. And as we answer to this demand, we gain a vivid sense of how Scripture gives life to the church.

There is neither complacency nor any sort of "theological" triumphalism in the presumption of accordance. On the contrary, to believe that what the church teaches accords with what the Bible says drives us away from the complacent doctrinalism in theology and the sterile historicism in biblical studies that we have tolerated for far too long. The bridge that needs building is from where we are now, from our current awakening to the inadequacy of many modern theological and interpretive practices, to the intellectually vibrant project of interpretation that restores a living relationship between doctrine and Scripture.

3

ORIGEN AND SPIRITUAL READING

ORIGEN WAS ONE OF CHRISTIAN antiquity's greatest figures. The most powerful reader of the Bible in the church's early centuries, he combined an intense focus on the details of Scripture with a stunning breadth of interpretive ambition. To read Origen's exegesis is like standing underneath a waterfall. Philological judgments, geographical clarifications, symbolic patterns, text-critical asides, doctrinal formulations, and allegorical schemes cascade down upon the reader. At the same time, his approach invariably pushes toward a unified reading of Scripture. In the opening sentence of Origen's seminal work, *On First Principles*, he tells us that his great speculative project has "no other source but the very words and teaching of Christ," words and teaching that are already present "in Moses and the prophets."[1] In this remarkable treatise, scriptural detail is married to an interpretive synthesis that reaches all the way to reflections on spirit and matter, time and eternity, the purpose of evil, the salvation of the devil, and the consummation of all things.

The effect can be disorienting. Either contemporary readers are thrilled by the scope and depth of Origen's approach or they

---

1. Origen, *On First Principles* 1.preface.1. Throughout I use the translation by G. W. Butterworth, reprinted as Origen, *On First Principles* (Gloucester, MA: Peter Smith, 1973).

worry about willfulness and overreach. The concreteness of the
literality of Scripture seems at odds with the abstractions of his
great theological system, and it is easy to think that the union
of the two in Origen's mind is forced and his approach to biblical interpretation arbitrary. A sensitive twentieth-century reader
of Origen, Maurice Wiles, took such a view. "In effect," Wiles
concludes, "Origen tries to have it both ways."[2] He wants a theological vision saturated with biblical particularity and yet universal
enough to encompass the great metaphysical questions of his day.
Contemporary readers like Wiles are not alone in their judgment
that Origen fails. Eusebius records Porphyry's assessment that
Origen was "in his life conducting himself as a Christian . . . , but
in his opinions of material things and of the Deity being like a
Greek, and mingling Grecian teachings with foreign fables."[3] This
negative assessment corresponds to the doubts Wiles harbors. And
although Origen has experienced a revival in recent decades, the
negative assessment retains currency to this day. Not a few university and seminary professors leave the impression that Origen
uses the material of Scripture to construct an intellectual edifice
according to Platonic principles.

I cannot provide a full defense of Origen against the charge that
he was playing cut and paste with Scripture in order to promote
Platonism with proof texts. To do so would require me to digress
into the implausibility of modern, foundationalist epistemologies
that rely on narrow "correspondence" theories of truth. These
theories treat certainty as our intellectual gold standard, holding
that evidence must match up directly with truth claims. To rebut
these theories and to debunk the idol of certainty, I would have to
draw upon Willard Quine's demonstration that our beliefs form

2. Maurice Wiles, "Origen as Biblical Scholar," in *The Cambridge History of
the Bible*, vol. 1, *From the Beginnings to Jerome*, ed. P. R. Ackroyd and C. F. Evans
(Cambridge: Cambridge University Press, 1970), 475.

3. Eusebius, *Ecclesiastical History* 6.19.7, in *A Select Library of Nicene and Post-
Nicene Fathers of the Christian Church*, 2nd series, ed. Philip Schaff and Henry Wace,
14 vols. (1890–1900; repr., Grand Rapids: Eerdmans, 1982), 1:266.

a complex web and cannot be reduced to one-to-one correspondences. I would also need to develop Imre Lakatos's account of scientific doctrine to explain how Christian doctrine has its roots in the great research project of patristic biblical interpretation that Origen did so much to advance.[4]

Rather than theorizing about Origen's exegetical practice in contemporary terms and judging it from afar, I propose that we enter into it. In this way, we can better appreciate his genius. And perhaps we will find that our assumptions about what counts as good exegesis are challenged. By bringing Origen's art of spiritual interpretation into focus, we can entertain the possibility that Porphyry underestimated the capacity of the "foreign fables" of Scripture to transform Greek ideas rather than the other way around. And if we will but consider this possibility—that the biblical text can absorb the world, not the world the text—we might find ourselves thinking fresh thoughts about how to develop fitting modes of spiritual interpretation for the twenty-first century.

———

In the final chapter of Luke's Gospel, the risen Jesus is portrayed walking with two men on the road to Emmaus. They are agitated by the events of Jesus's arrest, trial, and crucifixion. They encounter Jesus, but "their eyes were kept from recognizing him" (Luke 24:16). Jesus offers instruction: "Beginning with Moses and all the prophets, he interpreted to them the things about himself in all the scriptures" (24:27). This exposition is insufficient, or at least only partially effective. The two men continue to be inwardly blind, unable to recognize Jesus. But they implore the stranger who seems to know the Scriptures so well to stay with them.

4. To my mind, the best theoretical defense of the intellectual integrity of patristic exegesis is found in Khaled Anatolios, *Retrieving Nicaea: The Development and Meaning of Trinitarian Doctrine* (Grand Rapids: Baker Academic, 2011). Anatolios uses different philosophical sources than those I mention above, and he does not focus on Origen, but his analysis can be adapted to our topic.

Only after the risen Lord breaks bread with the two disciples are their eyes opened (Luke 24:30–31). They suddenly know why their hearts were burning within as Jesus was expounding the Scriptures to them on the road. He had been showing them that "all the scriptures" foretold that "the Messiah is to suffer and to rise from the dead on the third day, and that repentance and forgiveness of sins is to be proclaimed in his name to all nations" (24:46–47). With this knowledge, made real in the breaking of the bread, the disciples are prepared to be "clothed with power from on high" (24:49).

In their understanding of Scripture and its interpretation, the church fathers operated with the assumptions at work in this episode from Luke's Gospel. How are we to read so that our hearts might burn with desire for a deeper fellowship with the risen Christ?

Irenaeus of Lyons provided some of the key categories for the early Christian tradition, including Origen. He presumes that the Old Testament, however diverse in style and content, is a single text with a unified point or message. Using the terminology of the ancient rhetorical tradition, Irenaeus calls the unified message of Scripture its "hypothesis." At one level, he regards this hypothesis as literary. The Bible hangs together on its own terms, and readers sensitive to the hints and clues in the text will gravitate toward a unified reading. But more importantly, Irenaeus holds that the hypothesis of Scripture reflects the fact that the entire world is governed by a single divine plan, or "economy." This economy is constituted by a multilayered sequence of created realities, historical events, and divine ordinations and laws. In short, Irenaeus sees the entire world-process as a meaningful system shaped by God's saving intention. And, following Ephesians 1:10, Irenaeus argues that the complex facets of the divine economy, including the vast system of signs that make up the Old Testament, are recapitulated in Jesus Christ. Recapitulation (*anakephalaiōsis* in Greek) is another standard term in the ancient rhetorical tradition. In contemporary English we speak of ending a speech with a "recap," the conclusion in which the speaker drives home the theme with a restatement of the main arguments in pithy, vivid summary form.[5] According to Irenaeus (and he speaks for the Christian tradition as a whole), Christ is the basis and end point of the divine economy. He is the culminating summation of the divine speech ("And God said . . .") that brings forth reality.

According to Irenaeus (and the patristic tradition as a whole), God inspires the composition of the Bible in accord with his plan of salvation. How Scripture is so encoded remains obscure. There was no settled consensus in the early church about a doctrine of inspiration. Different views were held about the way in which Scripture expresses the overarching hypothesis that is recapitulated in Christ. But there was a consensus that the undeniable heterogeneity of Scripture—it says many things in many different ways—depicts a single divine economy. "If any one, therefore, reads the Scriptures with attention," writes Irenaeus, "he will find in them an account of Christ, and a foreshadowing of the new calling [of the gentiles]. For Christ was the treasure which was hid in the field, that is, in this world (for 'the field is the world' [Matt. 13:38]); but the treasure hid in the Scriptures is Christ, since He was pointed out by means of types and parables. Hence His human nature could not be understood, prior to the consummation of those things which had been predicted, that is, the advent of Christ."[6] The unity of Scripture grows out of the more fundamental singularity of God's purposes in and for all things, an economy directed toward fulfillment in Christ. Thus, the goal of exegesis is to bring Christ, the treasure hidden in the field of Scripture, into view. Doing so brings the reader to desire to live more fully in his truth.

5. For a helpful discussion of hypothesis, economy, and recapitulation, see R. M. Grant, *Irenaeus of Lyons* (London: Routledge, 1997), 47–51.

6. Irenaeus, *Against Heresies* 4.26.1, in *The Ante-Nicene Fathers: Translations of the Writings of the Fathers down to A.D. 325*, ed. Alexander Roberts and James Donaldson, 10 vols. (1885–87; repr., Grand Rapids: Eerdmans, 1978), 1:496.

In keeping with this larger patristic consensus, Origen sought to read Scripture in a Christ-signifying way. Commenting on the book of Joshua, Origen assembles a great deal of textual evidence to show that Joshua, successor to Moses, prefigures Jesus (whose name is identical in Greek). "To what then do all these things lead us?" Origen asks. His answer is a straightforward definition of spiritual exegesis: "Obviously to this, that the book does not so much indicate to us the deeds of the son of Nun, as it represents to us the mysteries of Jesus my Lord."[7] It is not the case that Origen thinks the book of Joshua is not about Joshua. The presumption of a divine economy culminating in Christ allows him to affirm the immediate textual references to Joshua *and* the orientation of the historical person of Joshua and the textual record of his deeds toward the larger purpose of fulfillment in Christ. It is Origen's assumption, as it is for the tradition he inherits, that the book of Joshua is filled with textual clues that, if followed correctly, bring Jesus more clearly into view, guiding our minds toward his truth.

Finding the treasure of Christ hidden in the field of Scripture is not always a straightforward enterprise. Not every biblical personage is as conveniently named as Joshua. Moreover, spiritual exegesis is a large-scale project, and it is rare that a particular interpretation will fully display the hypothesis of Scripture. Few interpretations are able to round out into explicitly christological conclusions. Preliminary approaches need to be made. The field of Scripture must be plotted and organized, and its treasure must be itemized and cataloged. It is in the execution of these detailed aspects of spiritual exegesis that Origen excels. Taking as his warrant 2 Timothy 3:16 ("All scripture is inspired by God and is useful for teaching, for reproof, for correction, and for training in righteousness"), Origen was justly famous in his own time for his ability to bring seemingly irrelevant and difficult biblical

7. Origen, *Homilies on Joshua*, trans. Barbara J. Bruce, Fathers of the Church 105 (Washington, DC: Catholic University of America Press, 2002), 29.

passages into the service of the overarching goal of discerning Christ in Scripture.

A good example can be found in his fifth homily on Exodus.[8] The biblical passage that serves as the basis for this homily is the description of the flight of the people of Israel from Egypt (Exod. 12:37ff.). Origen's interpretation exemplifies his remarkable combination of intense focus on literal detail with a penetrating theological synthesis.

Origen begins by reminding his listeners of Saint Paul's interpretation of Exodus in 1 Corinthians 10. Paul's reading involves an allegorical plotting of events onto core Christian beliefs and practices. The passage through the Red Sea is baptism; the manna from heaven corresponds to the eucharistic bread; the water from the rock that Moses struck with his rod suggests the eucharistic wine; and the rock indicates Christ himself. Origen reiterates this mapping of key elements of the exodus onto the central mysteries of the faith, reinforcing the Pauline reading with appeals to John 3:5 ("No one can enter the kingdom of God without being born of water and Spirit") and John 6:51 ("I am the living bread that came down from heaven"). But these remarks are preliminary. Paul, notes Origen, "taught the Church which he gathered from the Gentiles how it ought to interpret the books of the Law." Origen extends this approach so that "we, by understanding the Law spiritually, [can] show that it was justly given for the instruction of the Church."[9] With Paul's interpretive practice in mind, he urges, "Let us cultivate . . . the seeds of spiritual understanding received from the blessed apostle Paul."[10]

The great bulk of the verses that make up the story of the flight of the Israelites from Egypt concerns the baking of the unleavened bread, the divine commandments to remember the Passover,

---

8. Origen, *Homilies on Genesis and Exodus*, trans. Ronald E. Heine, Fathers of the Church 71 (Washington, DC: Catholic University of America Press, 1982), 275–84.

9. Origen, *Homilies on Genesis and Exodus*, 275.

10. Origen, *Homilies on Genesis and Exodus*, 277.

and the passage through the Red Sea. This material is rich with theological significance. But it is not Origen's focus. Instead, as if he were keen to find the smallest of seeds, Origen attends to the physical geography of the flight of the people of Israel.

> The children of Israel "departed," the text says, "from Ramesse and came to Socoth. And they departed from Socoth and came to Etham" [Exod. 12:37; 13:20]. If there is anyone who is about to depart from Egypt, if there is anyone who desires to forsake the dark deeds of this world and the darkness of errors, he must first of all depart "from Ramesse." *Ramesse* means "the commotion of a moth." Depart from Ramesse, therefore, if you wish to come to this place that the Lord may be your leader and precede you "in the column of the cloud" [Exod. 13:21] and "the rock" may follow you [1 Cor. 10:3–4], which offers you "spiritual food" and "spiritual drink" no less. Nor should you store treasure "there where the moth destroys and thieves dig through and steal" [Matt. 6:20]. This is what the Lord says clearly in the Gospels: "If you wish to be perfect, sell all your possessions and give to the poor, and you will have treasure in heaven; and come, follow me" [Matt. 19:21]. This, therefore, is to depart "from Ramesse" and to follow Christ.[11]

This reflection on the meaning of "Ramesse" is brief. As the homily proceeds, Origen follows the journey forward, performing similar exegetical reflection on the other place names mentioned in the Exodus account. But I want to tarry here, for this compact snapshot of Origen's exegesis provides us with more than enough material to enter into the logic of his way of reading Scripture.

The intensity with which Origen squeezes a sequence of scriptural connections out of the mere name "Ramesse" can lead us to conclude that he is spiritualizing the text so thoroughly that the words in Exodus (in this case a single word) exert no authority over his interpretation. One of the most influential anti-Origenist historians of the last century, R. P. C. Hanson, claims that al-

---

11. Origen, *Homilies on Genesis and Exodus*, 277.

legory (and by this term Hanson includes nearly all forms of spiritual exegesis) is "a technique for emancipating the exegete from bondage to the text."[12] Hanson holds Origen's approach to be an egregious example of interpretation unbound. The upshot is "arbitrary," "subjective," and "anti-historical" interpretation.[13] Few vituperate as boldly as does Hanson, but most modern readers assume that exegetical comments of this sort are but an occasion for Origen to retail some of his favorite verses from the New Testament.

I do not want to gainsay the feeling of anxiety when confronted with Origen's exegesis. But I reject the judgment that Origen is "imposing" meanings on the text. Consider the way in which his interpretation operates. Origen moves from "moth" in the meaning of the Hebrew place name "Ramesse" to "moth" in a verse on the Sermon on the Mount. The link is not purely semantic. Origen mentions the "dark deeds of this world," and although he does not make it explicit, the image of moths and their apparently futile and blind fluttering evokes the futile and blind grasping of men caught in the snares of worldly desire. "Moth" leads to "moth," and once the move is made, Origen quickly picks up the word "treasure," and with that verbal clue links the warning in Matthew 6:20 to Christ's positive exhortations to give to the poor and "come, follow me" (Matt. 19:21).

These moves are not arbitrary. A skein of images and verbal echoes holds the exegesis together. Origen is operating with the assumption that Irenaeus insists upon. Scripture bears witness to a sequence of events, people, places, and, in this case, Hebrew and Greek words that are part of the divine economy. All the particular elements play a role in a single, unified composition. They are pieces of a vast puzzle that awaits proper arrangement so that the call of discipleship can be heard anew. Origen does

12. R. P. C. Hanson, "Biblical Exegesis in the Early Church," in Ackroyd and Evans, *Cambridge History of the Bible*, 1:450.
13. Hanson, "Biblical Exegesis," 1:436.

not situate the textual elements in what modern readers might call a "historical context." Rather, the images, words, and verses are placed within the divine economy.[14] Origen moves from the place name "Ramesse" to the image of consuming moths in Matthew 6:20, to Jesus's exhortation to give to the poor in Matthew 19:21, to what could well serve as a summation of the entire New Testament: "Come, follow me." And he does so with a confidence that the verbal connections are not accidental. God in his providence has placed these clues in the text.

The clues in the field of Scripture lead toward the treasure hidden within: the crucified and risen Lord. We may not share this conviction with Irenaeus and Origen (and the Christian tradition until the modern period). But we should have sufficient intellectual integrity to recognize that the notion of a divine economy disciplines exegesis. Consider an analogy to scientific inquiry. Evolutionary biologists study the details of animal morphology and function. The data never manifest a smooth, self-evident line of evolution. Biologists must make connections in their analysis of species development, and these connections require "jumps" from one data point to another. What gives us confidence that these jumps are not arbitrary is that they fit into and reinforce the evolutionary hypothesis. If analysis is true to the facts, and if the analysis helps extend the interpretive reach of evolutionary theory, then we are inclined to accept biologists' reasoning as disciplined and objective rather than arbitrary and subjective.

The same holds for Origen. It will not do to object that he focuses on the place names while neglecting the narrative of Exodus any more than one might complain that a biologist is merely considering the mating behavior of frogs rather than their anatomy. An interpretation is a good interpretation if it supports and

14. For the use of the analogy of a mosaic that creates a picture of the "handsome king," see Irenaeus, *Against Heresies* 1.8–9. These crucial chapters are well explained by Rowan Greer in James L. Kugel and Rowan A. Greer, *Early Biblical Interpretation* (Philadelphia: Westminster, 1986), 155–76.

contributes to our understanding of the presumed hypothesis—and our hypothesis is sound insofar as it helps us arrange data in convincing and illuminating ways.

In his reflections on the departure from Ramesse, Origen is adding support to the larger patristic project of developing a total or overall reading of Scripture under the hypothesis that all things are recapitulated or summed up in Christ. Origen takes a seemingly irrelevant piece of scriptural data ("Ramesse") and interprets it toward the broad Christian imperative, "Come, follow me." The Hebrew meaning of "Ramesse" triggers a sequence of comments that culminate in Christ's saving invitation. He discerns the christological potency of a detail of Scripture and displays it in his exegesis.

But there is more. A discerning reader of this brief piece of exegesis can see that Origen is addressing a problem implicit in Saint Paul's interpretation of Exodus in 1 Corinthians. Paul's exegesis associates the rock with Christ, and the apostle observes that the rock (Christ) follows the Israelites (the baptized). For Origen, the words of Paul must be true, for they carry his apostolic authority. But they seem to contradict that biblical exhortation to *follow* Christ. Which, then, shall it be: Is Christ following behind us, or is he before us to be followed? Is he the Alpha, or is he the Omega?

Origen does not explicitly raise, much less resolve, this theological question in the small portion of exegesis we are analyzing. Instead, he supplements the Pauline scheme found in 1 Corinthians 10. The way in which Origen is able to end his skein of verbal association with the exhortation "Come, follow me" reinforces his observation that the Lord leads "in the column of the cloud" even as he follows as "the rock" to whom we may always return for the renewing nourishment of "spiritual food" and "spiritual drink." The words that drive the exegesis ("Ramesse," "moth," "treasure," "Come, follow me") flow in the same direction as the hypothesis of Scripture as a whole. Christ is both the firm foundation (not only in the ritual life of the church but as the *logos* of creation) and the final destination (not only as the pattern of self-sacrificial love but as the eternal Son of God). Thus, just as a biologist who publishes a paper on the mating behaviors of an obscure species of frogs in West Texas adds another brick to the edifice of evolutionary theory, Origen's reading of Ramesse contributes to the larger project of the Christian interpretation of Scripture.

One may object that the theological puzzle of Christ as Alpha and Omega is not to be found in this portion of Origen's exegesis, at least not explicitly. And the same person could note that I have done to Origen what Origen did to the literal sense of Exodus—pushed it beyond what it actually says. This objection brings us full circle and clarifies what is at stake in the exegesis. In the practice of Origen and the larger patristic tradition, interpretation is preparatory. The primary function of exegesis is to get us moving in the right direction. It cannot bring us to the destination the way a syllogism brings us to its conclusion. The end or goal of exegesis is to dispose the reader to "see" Christ. As the final chapter of Luke's Gospel makes clear, the disposing and the seeing are distinct.

———

The preparatory, disposing role of spiritual exegesis accounts for our feeling that it is indefinite, open-ended, and inconclusive. The reading for which Origen is so justly famous stretches toward the larger hypothesis of Scripture, preparing us for a further step, one that goes beyond the orderly exposition of commentary and toward faith's embrace of the truth of Christ. In this respect, Origen is extraordinarily well disciplined as an exegete. He does not offer exegetical conclusions of the sort one finds in modern readings of the Bible. He does not tell his readers the "theological" meaning of biblical passages—saying, for example, that the deliverance of the Israelites reveals the depths of God's love for humanity, or some other generalization. Instead, Origen pieces together the puzzle of Scripture in such a way that those reading his interpretations (or listening to them, as was the case in his day) are moved to take the next step. He disposes us to turn toward contemplation of the larger scheme of interlocking events, people, and words that come together in Christ.

Origen describes exegesis as a kind of construction that offers us promising vistas, not as an argument that leads to definite conclusions. Good biblical interpretation constructs a "house of reason, as it were," and it is built with proclamation and written characters in such a way that "God can add his free-cooperation to the projector of so noble a work."[15] Words such as "Ramesse" suggest other words such as "moth" and "treasure," which in turn suggest the spiritual disciplines of detaching oneself from worldly things and devoting one's life to following Christ. These are among the many bricks and beams with which we are to construct the house of interpretation. And this house is not the destination or end point of biblical interpretation. It is an edifice of signs erected by the interpreter in order for readers to be properly oriented and thus "capable of receiving the principles of truth."[16] The house of interpretation provides windows out of which to peer as we seek to contemplate God, which is the proper end of all intellectual activity, especially biblical exegesis. To recall the conclusion to the Gospel of Luke, biblical interpretation does not deliver truths in neat propositional packages; it prepares the reader to be clothed with power from on high.

For those who wish to learn from Origen, the test of exegesis is not its proximity to the literal sense of the Bible any more than the convincing character of evolutionary theory depends on its depiction of the specific morphology of frogs. Origen certainly

15. Origen, *Commentary on John* 6.1, in *The Ante-Nicene Fathers: Translations of the Writings of the Fathers down to A.D. 325*, ed. Alexander Roberts and James Donaldson, 10 vols. (1885–87; repr., Grand Rapids: Eerdmans, 1978), 10:349. See this first paragraph of book 6 of Origen's *Commentary on John* for his use of the metaphor of a house to describe his exegetical project.

16. Origen, *Commentary on John* 6.1.

wants to bring the literal sense of the Bible into focus, just as
scientists want to get their facts right. He learned Hebrew and
consulted with Jewish scholars in order to be informed about the
best available scholarly opinions about the meaning of words such
as "Ramesse." He compiled the most comprehensive text-critical
tool of antiquity, the *Hexapla*, so called because it was a manu-
script that arranged the Hebrew version of the Old Testament
along with five Greek translations in parallel columns. Getting
the facts right was clearly important to Origen. But the goal of
exegesis is interpretation, not description.

"The contents of scripture," writes Origen, "are the outward
forms of certain mysteries and the images of divine things."[17] The
true test of exegesis, like the test of any intellectually ambitious
interpretation, is whether our reading of the text brings us to see
what holds all the different pieces together. Just as fossils stand
as visible, embodied indications of the evolutionary economy
of natural selection, so also do the signs of Scripture manifest
the shaping intent of God, the divine economy of redemption
in Christ. The biologist wants us to see the process of natural
selection at work in the evolution of the tiniest of insects. Origen
wants us to see the redemptive love of God at work in even the
smallest details of Scripture.

Origen holds that the essential purpose of biblical exegesis
(and he does not differ from the rest of the early Christian tradition on this issue) is to guide the reader through the scriptural
text toward knowledge of the larger unity it depicts, and from
knowledge of that unity toward contemplation of the divine. For
this reason, his approach to interpretation (and, again, this accords with larger patristic tradition) will always strike us as "out
of control." For the most part, modern biblical interpreters do
not accept the hypothesis that all things are fulfilled in Christ,
and if they do, they think they must cordon off their faith from

17. Origen, *On First Principles* 1.preface.8.

their work as exegetes. As a result, modern traditions of exegesis build houses of interpretation that help us see the truth of worldly economies: the economy of ancient Israelite religion; the economy of "what really happened"; the economy of theological concepts that float about in the minds of the putative authors or redactors; or, if one has a postmodern bent, the economy of power, desire, and domination. In these and other ways, we fasten down scriptural texts onto our assumptions about how the world "really works." In truth, it is we—not Origen—who shy away from the text as text. Our ambition is to plot the Scriptures onto something more stable and more manageable than the world of signs that is always pointing to the divine compositor, the Author not just of Scripture but of our destinies. Because we presume that historical cause and effect are what count, finally, as determinative, our methods have a downward thrust rather than raising our eyes upward to the heavenly power overseeing all things. We "embody" the Bible rather than follow its spiritual sense. To "embody" is the metaphysical meaning of the modern interpretive ideal of putting scriptural texts into their historical and social contexts. Or we theorize Scripture, translating it into the idioms of systematic theology. Or we interpret in accord with a master concept such as patriarchy, another downward-looking trajectory that sees lust for power and domination as the world's true economy.

Origen moves in the other direction. He spiritualizes, not by trafficking in vague ideas or by directing attention to spiritual platitudes but, rather, in the very precise sense of constructing a reading of the words—the literal sense, their order, and their symbolic potential—that prepares us for contemplation of the mysteries of the Christian faith. As Origen wonders, "Who, on reading the revelations made to John, could fail to be amazed at the deep obscurity of the unspeakable mysteries contained therein, which are evident even to him who does not understand what is written? And as for the apostolic epistles, what man who is skilled in literary interpretation would think them to be plain and easily

understood, when even in them there are thousands of passages
that provide, as if through a window, a narrow opening leading
to multitudes of the deepest thoughts?"[18] Origen's goal was not
to use his pen (or, more accurately, the pens of the secretaries
who transcribed his homilies and lectures) to pass through the
narrow opening. This is what each of us must do with our own
thoughts and prayers. Origen aimed at good exegesis that frames
the windows and brings us to their sills. It stimulates our desire to
look out upon divine reality, preparing us to respond to Christ's
invitation: "Come, follow me."

Origen was an exegetical virtuoso, but he was a virtuoso within
a consensus. Where he innovated was in his speculative theology.
Some of his innovations became controversial and subsequently
tainted the name of Origen with heresy.[19] But my interest does not
lie in Origen's reflections on the salvation of the devil, which later
generations judged wrongheaded. Rather, I wish to focus on his
account of Scripture and exegesis outlined in book 4 of *On First
Principles*. In this material, Origen casts a fresh and interesting
light on the role of the literal sense of Scripture in the divine plan.
He gives spiritual meaning to the labor of exegesis, showing how

18. Origen, *On First Principles* 4.2.3.
19. See Jerome's list of Origenist errors in his letter to Avitus (*Epistle* 124.1–15).
Jerome was scrupulous about orthodoxy and ecclesiastical censure. It is telling that
he conveyed many of Origen's exegetical insights to the Latin-speaking world even
as he entered the lists as an adversary of Origenism. Origen's exegetical work was so
instrumental in the consolidation of what became the dominant orthodox tradition
that it necessarily endured, even as his name came to be associated, in part, with
doctrinal error. For a helpful account of the first wave of Origenist controversies in
the late fourth and early fifth centuries, with special focus on the monastic context,
see William Harmless, *Desert Christians: An Introduction to the Literature of Early
Monasticism* (New York: Oxford University Press, 2004), 359–63. For a fuller account,
see Elizabeth Clark, *The Origenist Controversy: A Cultural Construction of an Early
Christian Debate* (Princeton: Princeton University Press, 1992). For a winsome and
sympathetic description of Origen's systematic project, see Rowan Williams, "Origen," in *The First Theologians*, ed. G. R. Evans (Oxford: Blackwell, 2003).

the effort necessary to build an enduring house of interpretation provides fitting ascetic discipline, an exegetical *via crucis* for faithful readers. But before turning to book 4, I need to explain Origen's account of the blessing of embodiment. For the literal sense of Scripture—its embodiment in linguistic signs—functions as an important aspect of this blessing.

Origen employs a vocabulary and pattern of thought that derives from Platonic philosophy. It was this influence that gave rise to Porphyry's misconception (shared by many modern scholars) that Origen holds a Platonic view of the nature and fate of our embodiment. This is not the case. Origen offers a biblically informed account of the body that differs significantly from the Platonic view, which regards the body as an impediment to the spiritual life, a dead weight that burdens the divine spark within. Origen, by contrast, considers the advantages of bodily existence. As he observes, bodies are plastic and capable of transformation.[20] The body's vulnerability to change provides God with an avenue of influence that can guide and shape our lives without coercing or controlling our wills. In a crucial passage, Origen observes, "The bodily nature admits of a change in substance, so that God the Artificer of all things, in whatever work of design or construction or restoration he may wish to engage, has at hand the service of this material for all purposes, and can transform and transfer it into whatever forms and species he desires, as the merits of things demand."[21] In short, embodiment is a blessing—a decidedly non-Platonic conclusion. Our flesh makes us subject to the divinely ordained economy that is ordered toward our redemption in Christ.

Speaking of embodiment as a blessing seems counterintuitive because very often we experience the economy of our flesh as pain and suffering. We thirst and hunger. We get sick. We age and grow feeble. We die. The key point for Origen is that God so orders and

20. See Origen, *On First Principles* 2.1.4.
21. Origen, *On First Principles* 3.6.7.

arranges the created world that our bodily suffering encourages us to direct our attention toward the divine. Thus, in *On First Principles*, the world-process is conceived of as a pedagogy of bodies. True, it is subjectively experienced as "very severe and no doubt full of pain to those who have refused to obey the word of God."[22] But in truth the economy of created reality is objectively ordered toward "instruction and training whereby through the flesh the human race, aided by the heavenly powers, is being instructed and trained."[23] This training engages us as finite, embodied beings subject to suffering, a word in the Greek used by Origen that also means being subject to change. "We must recognize," writes Origen, "that the world was made of such a size and character as to be able to hold all those souls which were destined to undergo discipline in it."[24] God, the artificer of all things, sets up the created order so that we undergo an ascetic therapy of suffering. Such is the grace of our embodied finitude.

In this account (which occupies books 1–3 of *On First Principles*), Origen develops a metaphysical interpretation of Irenaeus's sequential or temporal notion of a divine economy that governs events. Viewed from a cosmological rather than salvation-historical perspective, God has established an economy of bodily existence that puts pressure on us, a pressure we experience as suffering. This pressure drives us upward, toward the spiritual. The fact that we suffer from illnesses and encounter the reality of death, for example, does not necessarily distract us from spiritual truths. On the contrary, as we often notice in ourselves and others, the pangs of finitude goad us toward our true end, which is contemplation of things higher than our mortal existence.

The same holds for the literal sense of Scripture. The ascetic economy of Scripture follows the ascetic economy of creation. God has arranged the words of Scripture in such a way that the

22. Origen, *On First Principles* 1.6.3.
23. Origen, *On First Principles* 2.3.1.
24. Origen, *On First Principles* 3.5.4.

literal sense pressures readers toward the spiritual sense. The semantic code of the Bible does not just teach the truth about the
divine economy; the literality of Scripture embodies the way of
the cross. To suffer the literal sense of Scripture drives the reader
toward Christ—if the reader will but follow the words where they
lead.[25]

In the prologue to his *Commentary on the Song of Songs*,
Origen explains the pedagogy of the literal sense. He follows the
church fathers more generally by pointing out that we need to
undergo ascetic discipline that purifies our desires in order to avoid
carnal titillation. Readers who have failed to gain control over their
sexual desires are very likely to dwell upon the erotic images of
the racy love poetry of the Song of Songs. However, Origen goes
a step farther. He identifies a disciplining logic within the text
itself. In the case of the Song of Songs, he dwells on the order of
the three books ascribed to Solomon: Proverbs, Ecclesiastes, and
Song of Songs.

The first, he reports, concerns "the subject of morals, setting regulations for life together, as was fitting, in concise and
brief maxims." To use Origen's categories, Proverbs is a bodily
book in which the literal sense guides readers on the right path
toward righteousness. The second, Ecclesiastes, provides instruction about "natural things," and "by distinguishing them
as empty and vain from what is useful and necessary, [Solomon]
warns that vanity must be abandoned and what is useful and
right must be pursued."[26] The second book of Solomon is thus
taken by Origen to be philosophical. It is written at the level of

25. On the ascetic economy of theological inquiry, see John Henry Newman's
Grammar of Assent (Notre Dame, IN: University of Notre Dame Press, 1979). Newman is not concerned specifically with biblical interpretation, but his assessment
of the difficulties follows Origen's. God, writes Newman, "has made this path of
thought rugged and circuitous above other investigation, that the very discipline
inflicted on our minds in finding Him, may mould them in due devotion to Him
when He is found" (276).

26. Origen, *Commentary on the Song of Songs*, in *Origen*, trans. Rowan A. Greer
(New York: Paulist Press, 1979), 232.

the soul, providing guidance toward the right path, not in each verse according to the literal sense, but in the book's overall demonstration of the vanity of temporal things. According to Origen, these two books are providentially placed before Song of Songs in the canon of Scripture because the reader must pass through these stages of spiritual development in order to properly read the third and final book of Solomon. In this way, the very order of the books in Scripture provides a pedagogy of interpretation, bringing readers through a process that makes them capable of properly interpreting the spiritual sense of the Bible's famous love poem.

The trajectory of this pedagogy is toward the spiritual. But as Origen makes clear in his discussion of bodily existence in *On First Principles*, our ascent is not undertaken in spite of or against the grain of bodily existence. God induces spiritual growth in and through bodily suffering. Origen strikes the same note in his account of the pedagogy of Scripture in book 4 of *On First Principles*. The paths of Scripture do not always ascend happily from level to level, as his account of the relationship between Proverbs, Ecclesiastes, and Song of Songs would seem to suggest. The meaning and order of words in Scripture are often full of puzzles and difficulties. What are we to make of strange place names such as "Ramesse"? Building the house of interpretation is arduous and afflicts us with uncertainty. Is our reading accurate? Are our interpretations true to God's Word? But the Author of the economy of Scripture has made it so that we will not suffer unnecessarily. The burdens of interpretation force us to take the narrow way, which is a blessing, for the wide way leadeth to destruction.

"Divine wisdom," Origen observes, "has arranged for certain stumbling blocks and interruptions of the historical sense . . . by inserting in the midst a number of impossibilities and incongruities, in order that the very interruption of the narrative might as it were present a barrier to the reader and lead him to refuse to

proceed along the pathway of the ordinary meaning."[27] He goes on
to assemble a great list of passages from Scripture that illustrate
the pain imposed by the literal sense. Some are patently "mytho-
logical" or anthropomorphic (e.g., the passage in Genesis that
speaks of God walking in paradise). Some are culturally limited
(Jesus's commandment to his disciples not to own shoes). And
some are morally repugnant (a verse in the Septuagint that would
seem to require uncircumcised boys to be destroyed).[28] Origen
points out how difficult it is to read the elaborate Old Testament
instructions for the construction and decoration of the tabernacle
as significant for Christian faith. Working out a Christian reading
of this material in any detail is "a very difficult, not to say impossible task."[29] He could have adduced many more examples. The
stumbling blocks of Scripture are many.

Origen does not advance a view of scriptural authority that
treats the Bible as a collection of propositions to be deployed as
premises in doctrinal syllogisms or called out as trumps in theological arguments. He agrees with modern historical critics. The
particular senses of Scripture are recalcitrant, difficult, and obscure. If the interpreter believes that Scripture is the divine Word
(as Origen clearly does, as all Christians must), then sometimes,
perhaps often, the result will be a painful grimace of suffering. It
is as if Origen had anticipated the experience of pious students
who, having enrolled in a course in biblical studies, are confronted
by a professor who spends a great deal of time showing just how
badly the Bible fits with their inherited faith.

This experience of disorientation can evoke a Job-like question.
Why has God organized his witness in such a way that the more
I learn about the Bible, the more difficult it is to make sense of it?
According to Origen, the answer is spiritual. To know the lan-
guages, to be capable of memorizing the text, to have a powerful

27. Origen, *On First Principles* 4.2.9.
28. See Origen, *On First Principles* 4.3.1.
29. Origen, *On First Principles* 4.2.2.

intellect, and even to possess the rule of faith is not enough. We interpret truly when our reading of Scripture brings us to see the mystery of God. But our carnal eyes cannot see the luminous holiness of God. To overcome our carnality, the literal sense of Scripture humiliates us. The Bible stymies our interpretive efforts so that "by shutting us out and debarring us from [literal reading, it] recalls us to the beginning of another way, and might thereby bring us, through the entrance of a narrow footpath, to a higher and loftier road and lay open the immense breadth of the divine wisdom."[30] Reading the Bible is difficult because God wants us to pant with desire for insight. He wants us to become the kind of person "who has devoted himself to studies of this kind with the utmost purity and sobriety and through nights of watching."[31] We must suffer in dry deserts of incomprehension so that, disciplined by the recalcitrance of Scripture, our vision will be sanctified and we will be prepared to ascend by the narrow footpath.

Origen's reflections on the nature of Scripture and its interpretation should inform today's much-needed project of theological interpretation. We must renounce our desire for "solutions" to the great crossword puzzle of Scripture. "The Spirit has mingled not a few things by which the historical narrative is interrupted and broken," Origen writes, anticipating modern judgments about the historical inaccuracy of Scripture. But he does not adopt the modern effort to domesticate interpretation by anchoring it in stable, extrabiblical contexts, be they historical, phenomenological, conceptual, or postmodern. Instead, he embraces Scripture's interruptions, incongruities, immoralities, and contradictions as divine gifts that require us to stretch and reach toward comprehension. This is why his spiritual reading can seem so strained.

Can it be otherwise? Who imagines that seeing the crucified Christ as the risen Lord won't require stretching, reaching, and

30. Origen, *On First Principles* 4.2.9.
31. Origen, *On First Principles* 4.2.7.

straining? It was so for the disciples on the road to Emmaus. God has sown difficulty into the fields of Scripture "with the object of turning and calling the attention of the reader, by the impossibility of the literal sense, to an examination of the inner meaning."[32] God ordains the difficulties of interpretation not so that we might solve "problem texts," after the fashion of a murder mystery or a math problem, but so that difficult texts might focus our minds and lives on a solution that cannot be arrived at or possessed as a conclusion to an argument—seeing the face of Christ. Origen anticipates in his theology of Scripture and its difficulties what Saint Augustine articulates in his theology of grace. The roadblocks to interpretation—Scripture's heterogeneity, its contradictions and ambiguities, its historical layers and textual variants—are grace-given. We are driven through the "narrow openings" of Scripture so that we might "be flooded with the brightness of immeasurable light."[33]

———

My sense is that many contemporary Christian readers of Origen (and of this book) tend to find him appealing. As I have noted, he has undergone a revival of sorts. His biblical interpretation is inventive and mobile. His eye for telling detail is keen. And the forward strain of his exegetical practice has an adventuresome, heroic quality. But the excitement we feel while reading Origen is difficult to translate into a consensus for the future of Christian interpretation of the Bible. Reading from the obscure place name "Ramesse" to the great New Testament invitation "Come, follow me" seems impossible for us to imitate. Which raises an important question: Why does the tradition of spiritual interpretation that Origen so ably represents remain remote and inimitable?

32. Origen, *On First Principles* 4.2.9.
33. Origen, *On First Principles* 4.2.3. Compare this with Augustine's own image of the divine pedagogy of signs that we are to use for the sake of enjoyment of God and others in God in *On Christian Doctrine*, book 1.

We are trained to say that a great chasm separates us from the church fathers. We know about *history*! The more I think about it, the less satisfied I am by this explanation. The church fathers presumed that Moses wrote the Pentateuch. We have good reasons to regard this presumption as wrong. We have monographs ready at hand that itemize parallels between aspects of the Pentateuch and other ancient Near Eastern religions. Treatises speculate about the original communal setting for the book of Exodus. Libraries are full of studies that discuss the Bible in its historical context, studies unavailable to the church fathers.

The modern tradition of historical study of the Bible makes a difference in some areas of biblical exegesis, to be sure. But when I turn to Origen's comment on Exodus 12:37 and consider the logic of his interpretation, I am at a loss to see what difference our modern historical consciousness makes. A certain desire for precision might lead me to say "the place from which the final form of Exodus says the Israelites departed" rather than "the place from which the Israelites departed." This would signal that I am not assuming the book of Exodus to be a straightforward, eyewitness account of what happened. Yet, once signaled, why would my mind not follow Origen's train of thought? I can read scholarly articles explaining how redaction criticism helps us understand the relationship between the narrative of Israel's flight and the instructions for the observance of the Passover. With the strands of the text separated and analyzed, I might have new and subtle thoughts about the meaning of the twelfth chapter of Exodus. But why would these new thoughts not contribute to, rather than contradict, Origen's pattern of textual analysis? What is it about *history* that blocks an interpretive move from "Ramesse" to "moths" to a reported saying of Jesus, "Come, follow me"?

The crucial assumption that supports Origen's bold exegetical moves is a belief in the divine economy. It rests in the conviction that God has the power to arrange the great diversity of Scripture—including the complexities of the Bible's composition—in accord with his overarching hypothesis. If one believes that God providentially orders all things toward fulfillment in Christ (as did Origen, and we should as well), then one has a warrant for discerning this providential order in every aspect of reality—including in place names recorded in Scripture, however we understand the process by which those place names became canonical in the final form of Scripture. I see no reason why the insights gained from modern historical study should not be understood *within* the divine economy. What cannot be accommodated is the modern economy of historical immanence. This economy insists that all human events are caused and structured by inner-worldly factors, to the exclusion of the divine economy.

We are not only taught the intellectual techniques of historical-critical study, some of which can bear good fruit. We are also socialized into the modern economy of historical immanence, which contradicts our faith. This ill-starred socialization is why we regard the move from "Ramesse" to "Come, follow me" as arbitrary. Imbued by the modernist assumption that historical causality is what makes things "really real," we conclude that there is no reason to think that these bits of text are linked "in reality." There is no *historical* connection. Origen thought otherwise. He supposed that God structures reality, not the "laws of history." The divine economy includes the words of the Bible. God orders the signs of Scripture with an eye toward disciplining those who desire to see his face. Origen moved from "Ramesse" to "Come, follow me" because he saw a *spiritual* connection, which, given the reality of God, is more "real" than any historical connections we might discern. If we mistrust what Origen sees, then in all likelihood it's because we're not confident that God exists. And even if we allow that God does exist, we don't believe he supervises all things in accord with his redemptive plan.

"If anyone ponders over [the Scriptures] with all the attention and reverence they deserve," Origen writes, "it is certain that in the very act of reading and diligently studying them his mind and

feelings will be touched by a divine breath and he will recognize
that the words he is reading are not utterances of man but the
language of God."[34] What separates us from Origen is not his
supposed lack of "historical consciousness." Were we to presume
the Scriptures to be the language of God, I am confident we would
be able to retain many of the insights of modern historical-critical
study. For belief in God's providence entails belief in his power
to order the strange, diverse, complex, historically layered, and
even seemingly contradictory witness of the Bible in such a way
that, taken as a whole, it testifies to a coherent—nay, beautiful and
holy—plan. To actually believe in God's providence rather than
"laws of history"—this may be a difficult ditch to leap over. But
I see no reason, other than the deeply parochial modernism that
dominates our increasingly tired and decadent academic culture,
why we cannot do so.

34. Origen, *On First Principles* 4.1.6.

4

REFORMATION CONTROVERSY AND BIBLICAL INTERPRETATION

MARTIN LUTHER OVERSAW the publication of an edition of the New Testament for which he provided the translation. In his preface, Luther explains his reading of the New Testament as a whole. There is, he says, a canon within the canon, a center that "shows" Christ and his saving truth. Luther names John's Gospel and his first letter, the letters of Paul to the Romans, Galatians, and Ephesians, and Peter's first letter as the central texts that bear witness to the gospel. The Epistle of James is not part of that center. This letter is on the periphery, for, as Luther says, "it has nothing of the nature of the gospel about it."[1] It is, as he put it, an "*epistola straminea*" (epistle of straw), and Luther appended James, along with Hebrews, Jude, and Revelation, to the end of the New Testament, among the "disputed books."

There can be little doubt that the Reformation doctrine of justification by faith determined Luther's negative assessment of James. Luther famously added an "alone" (*allein durch den Glauben*) to his translation of Romans 3:28: "We hold that a

1. *Luther's Works*, ed. Ernest Theodore Bachmann and Helmut T. Lehmann, vol. 35, *Word and Sacrament I* (Philadelphia: Fortress, 1970), 362.

man is justified by faith *alone* apart from works of law" (RSV alt.). This interpolation of "alone" into Paul's statement about justification turned the verse into a clear statement of Luther's own view, which made for an even more pointed contradiction of James 2:24: "A man is justified by works and not by faith alone" (RSV).

Luther was not the only Reformation interpreter who anguished over the apparent affirmation of works righteousness in the Epistle of James. In the century following Luther's translation of the Bible, interpretive debates about James were highly charged with concerns about the doctrine of justification. The evident role of doctrinal commitments in these disputations about the exegesis of James (and the Pauline Letters) raises a question in the minds of most modern readers: In the premodern period, did doctrine overdetermine interpretation? Don't we want Scripture to speak for itself rather than being manhandled to fit into preconceived dogmatic schemes?

As I've noted before, the concern seems reasonable. Who wouldn't want the Bible to speak for itself? But I wonder whether our assumptions about "objective" interpretation are accurate. Does close attention to doctrine invariably flatten out Scripture, making it serve as a source of proof texts for dogmas? The evidence suggests otherwise. As I hope to show in this brief survey of Reformation-era readings of James, the influence of doctrine heightened rather than diminished interpretive attention. Instead of "silencing" the text, a sense of the vital importance of doctrine triggered interpretive ambition. The Reformation debate about justification serves as a case study of the promise of theological exegesis. Dogmatic commitments put pressure on sixteenth-century interpreters, both Protestant and Catholic. They were driven to dig deeply into the biblical text, developing subtle exegetical strategies in order to sustain their doctrinal convictions. The result was exegetical innovation, in some cases anticipating the central insights of modern historical-critical interpretation.

As I have sought to show throughout these reflections, premodern exegesis does not treat doctrine as a premise in exegetical arguments, nor does it arrive at conclusions drawn from interpretation done by other means. Instead, doctrine establishes interpretive priorities, providing what might be called a "horizon of truth" that focuses exegesis rather than dictating results. Doctrinal commitments do not make things easy for the faithful reader. They force us to think through the details of Scripture.

As I observed in the previous chapter, Irenaeus insists that the Bible as a whole has a hypothesis. Scripture speaks of the crucified and risen Christ in and through the many things it says. To explain how the hypothesis works, Irenaeus offers the analogy of a mosaic. It starts out as a collection of many small tiles in a wide array of colors. Were we merely to spread them before us, we'd be at a loss as to their proper order. The same holds for the great diversity of the Bible. But the great Maker of the scriptural mosaic has provided readers with a schematic drawing of the picture that the many tiles were fabricated to represent. The mosaic is meant to depict a "handsome king," says Irenaeus. The task of interpretation thus is to sift through the individual tiles, pondering their places within the larger scheme. Composing this entire mosaic piece by piece, verse by verse, book by book requires immense intellectual creativity, which is why, contrary to modern presumptions, doctrinal commitments outlining the larger truths of our faith—doctrines that teach us of the salvation offered by the handsome king—vivify rather than dull our reading of Scripture.

Let us begin with the way in which Luther approaches James. The problem is apparent. James seems to say that Abraham is justified by his works. But in his Letter to the Romans, Paul says the opposite. James describes the law as the power of liberty, while Paul describes the law as sin, slavery, and death. Here, we must sympathize with Luther. He faces a serious difficulty as he tries

to assemble the mosaic of Scripture. James seems peripheral, a
tile that provides background, at best, rather than playing a direct
role in depicting the handsome king, the main features of whom
are provided by the core New Testament texts, which Luther reads
as teaching justification by faith alone, the doctrine that sums up
the gospel of God's saving grace in the death and resurrection of
Christ. The fact that James is in the New Testament canon prevents Luther from simply dispensing with this troublesome text.
But he is eager to block any backsliding into works righteousness,
which is why he augmented Paul's affirmation in Romans of justification by faith by adding "alone." But this is not sufficient. Luther
must interpret James so that the epistle's irksome endorsement
of "works" can be brought into accord with what he takes to be
the normative teaching of the New Testament: justification by
faith alone.

In his preface to the Epistle of James, Luther's argument moves
along two tracks. First, he questions the apostolic status of James.
He observes that the epistle is not a tightly organized document.
Rather (and here he sounds like a modern historical critic), the
final form of James appears to be a loosely organized collection of apostolic sayings that were preserved by a postapostolic
writer. This judgment clears the way for Luther to assert that
Paul's Epistle to the Romans was written during the apostolic
age, while the Epistle of James is a later work, useful and in-
structive for the faithful, perhaps, but possessing significantly less
authority.

Luther's second line of argument also foreshadows modern
judgments about biblical texts. He speculates that the Epistle of
James was composed in a post-Pauline context. The *Sitz im Leben*
(the technical term from historical criticism that means the immediate social context of the text's composition and reception)
was a community in which antinomian readings of the doctrine of
justification by faith had gained credence. Against this misread-
ing of Paul (whose letters were composed at an earlier time, as

Luther tries to establish in his first line of argument), the author of James (who, as Luther has argued, is the redactor of a collection of apostolic sayings handed down) offers an unfortunately exaggerated and one-sided corrective to the notion that "faith alone" means that one need not worry about morality.

My purpose is not to assess the persuasiveness of Luther's analysis. I wish only to point out that his mind was stimulated to think through the question of canonical development and historical context *because of* the pressure created by his convictions about true doctrine. Instead of "imposing" the doctrine of justification by faith onto the Epistle of James, Luther's certainty that justification by faith alone captures the essential teaching of Scripture—the "handsome king" in doctrinal form—forces him to engage the text in subtle and creative ways that sharpen his historical vision. Basic forms of historical-critical analysis are suggestively hinted at as Luther seeks to maintain the *sola fide* doctrine over against the apparent works righteousness taught in the Epistle of James.

A second-generation Lutheran, Martin Chemnitz, gives further and more detailed evidence that attention to historical context and development was at this juncture doctrinally motivated. (I submit that historical criticism remained theologically motivated throughout the modern period, but that's a topic for a different book.) In his great work of dogmatics, *Loci Theologici*, Chemnitz discusses the doctrine of justification. Before launching into theological analysis, he offers an extended reflection on the history of salvation. As befits a man whose life was defined by the increasingly intractable conflict between Protestants and Roman Catholics over the definition of salvation, Chemnitz sees the entire history of humanity, from Adam and Eve to his own time, as shaped by disagreements about the doctrine of justification. Abel, he argues, anticipated the Reformation view, regarding his sins as lifted from his shoulders by faith in the promise of Christ, while Cain foreshadowed the Catholic view "that he could by his own sacrifices and other works remove and take away his sin."[2]

Chemnitz traces this history of justification by faith at war with works righteousness through the Old Testament, and he uses the same pattern of divergence to explain the structure of the New Testament, including the emphasis on works that we find in James. According to Chemnitz, the coming of Christ clarifies that justification comes through faith alone and not through the works of the law. At this point, with true doctrine so clearly and authoritatively defined, the devil must change strategies. Unable to defeat faith by proclaiming works, writes Chemnitz, "the devil foisted Epicurean philosophy [this term is Chemnitz's way of describing the antinomian rejection of moral constraints] upon the church."[3] The devil's new strategy explains the emphasis on works in the Epistle of James. "From this," writes Chemnitz, "we find a difference in the writing of the apostles, so that the earlier epistles are contending against the spirit of belief in the righteousness of the Law, while the later ones are promoting the fruits of repentance and refuting Epicurean notions regarding licentious living."[4]

Chemnitz is following Luther's pattern of analysis. The Pauline Letters come first. They teach what Christ taught. The Epistle of James comes a generation or two later, opposing demonically inspired antinomian misreadings of Paul's teaching of justification by faith alone. (Antinomianism was not uncommon in Luther and Chemnitz's own time.) James is therefore to be read as a secondary, corrective text rather than as a primary witness to the gospel. Paul's account of the proper ordering of law and gospel is authoritative and timeless. James's teaching is derivative and historically conditioned.

2. Martin Chemnitz, *Loci Theologici*, trans. J. A. O. Preus (St. Louis: Concordia, 1989), 2:463.
3. Chemnitz, *Loci Theologici*, 2:466.
4. Chemnitz, *Loci Theologici*, 2:466.

One rarely reads a contemporary writer discussing the historical development of the New Testament canon in terms of demonic plots, although the concept of patriarchy so cherished by many feminist interpreters is not all that different. But of this we can be sure: Chemnitz manifests a historical consciousness. Far from "imposing" the doctrine of justification, he develops a theory about the development of the New Testament canon that accords with his horizon of truth. The doctrine of justification clearly defines this horizon, and it plays a central role in stimulating his theory of development. Chemnitz is confident that it is an essential doctrine. Thus, when faced with the textual reality of the Epistle of James, he needs to explain how its seemingly contradictory teaching fits into a larger picture of New Testament proclamation of "faith alone." The upshot is historical speculation that describes the authorship of the texts of the New Testament in light of varying communal contexts. Paul is addressing the central theological question of how we are saved, while James is guarding against Epicurean (antinomian) distortions that corrupt Pauline teaching. The intellectual payoff is obvious. Establishing the historical priority of Paul and the *Sitz im Leben* for James allows for a doctrinally unified reading of the New Testament as a whole, one that sustains the Protestant view of justification by faith alone.

Not all Reformation interpreters used historical speculation to resolve the apparent conflict between Paul and James. In his commentary on the Epistle of James, Calvin adopts a scholastic device to read James in a way that is consistent with Paul's affirmation of justification by faith. Calvin's analysis turns on a distinction between two different senses of "faith." On the one hand, faith can mean what Calvin describes as "a bare and frigid knowledge of God."[5] This is belief, perhaps, but it is not a saving faith. Faith in a fuller sense means trust that brings us to participate in Christ.

5. John Calvin, *Commentaries on the Catholic Epistles*, trans. John Owen (Grand Rapids: Eerdmans, 1959), 310.

By Calvin's reckoning, the author of James was faced with adversaries who claimed that mere intellectual knowledge of Christ is sufficient. To combat them, he adopted the rhetorical trope of concession. "OK," if I might paraphrase Calvin's analysis, "you say you have faith, but were it true faith, it would manifest the Spirit of Christ." With this gloss, Calvin is able to preserve the plain sense of James in concert with a Reformation interpretation of Paul. When James says that Abraham is justified by his works, he is not contradicting Paul, who says Abraham is justified by his faith, not works. The two authors are using the word "faith" differently. Paul teaches the basic truth that by faith (understood as life-transforming trust) we are justified, "but James has quite another thing in view, to show that he who professes that he has faith [understood as mere intellectual cognition], must prove the reality of his faith by his works."[6]

I wish to emphasize yet again that doctrine does not short-circuit interpretation. It puts pressure on the reader and imposes a stringent demand: "Sort this out!" Calvin does not speculate about the historical context for the Epistle of James. Instead, he adds nuance to doctrine. We think we know what we mean when we say that we are justified by faith alone. But Calvin draws attention to the fact that faith can mean "bare and frigid" knowledge, which is very different from the kind of knowing that is participatory and grounded in trust. Thus, Calvin's approach runs counter to the cliché claim that church doctrine will lead one to "impose" a reading. The text of the Epistle of James pressures him to clarify a key theological concept—faith. In so doing, Calvin deepens our understanding of doctrine.

―――――

After the Reformation, the Catholic tradition developed its own teaching on faith and works, with obvious implications for how

6. Calvin, *Catholic Epistles*, 314.

we read the passages that exercised Luther, Chemnitz, and Calvin. Session 6 of the Council of Trent treats the doctrine of justification. Reading the session in its entirety, one cannot escape the impression that Trent flips the priority established by the Reformers. The Epistle of James serves as the governing center of Tridentine New Testament interpretation, while Paul's epistles offer addenda and supplementation.

Consider the way Trent quotes Paul. In chapter 7 of session 6, the bishops at Trent define justification as participation in Christ. (This corresponds to Calvin's definition of the true faith that justifies.) Our salvation in Christ is made possible by the infusion, by grace, of the virtues of faith, hope, and love. "For which reason," Trent concludes in the spirit of James 2:26, "it is most truly said, that Faith without works is dead and profitless." Immediately, Paul (Gal. 5:6) is brought into the argument as a supporting voice: "In Christ Jesus neither circumcision, availeth anything, nor uncircumcision, but faith which worketh by charity."[7] This use of Paul is characteristic of Trent. In the council's statements about justification, the independent clause is a paraphrase of James while the dependent clause comes from Paul. Here is a typical example: "The just themselves ought to feel themselves the more obligated to walk in the way of justice [a formulation akin to James 2:24], in that, being already freed from sins, but made servants of God [Rom. 6:22], they are able, living soberly, justly, and Godly [Titus 2:12], to proceed onwards through Jesus Christ, by whom they have had access unto this grace [Rom. 5:2]."[8] Elsewhere, Trent quotes passages in which Paul emphasizes growth in faith (see 1 Cor. 9:24ff.) and divine judgment according to our deeds (see Rom. 2:6), as well as many passages in which Paul condemns immoral acts and exhorts his reader to seek perfection. In sum: Trent

7. "General Council of Trent: Sixth Session," ed. and trans. J. Waterworth, Papal Encyclicals Online, "Decree on Justification," chapter 7, https://www.papalencyclicals.net/councils/trent/sixth-session.htm.
8. "General Council of Trent: Sixth Session," "Decree on Justification," chapter 11.

on justification holds that Paul's epistles reinforce the notion that faith without works is dead.

While Trent reads Paul as subordinate to James, the council does not offer an exegetical explanation; it simply pursues a strategy of quotation. For a Catholic account of the priority of James over Paul, we turn to R. P. Cornelius à Lapide, an influential Flemish Jesuit who, in the decades following the Council of Trent, wrote commentaries on nearly all the books of the Bible.

Lapide draws attention to the historical context for Paul's teachings against works righteousness. He notes that Paul is concerned about circumcision and other aspects of Jewish ceremonial law. By Lapide's reading, "Although the Jews perceived that they were justified by circumcision and the ceremonies prescribed by the Mosaic law, Paul rejects this, and teaches that all these things are insufficient and useless for justification and salvation without the faith and grace of Christ."[9] Lapide is inverting the Protestant position represented by Luther, Chemnitz, and Calvin. They read James as addressing a limited problem—the Epicurean subplot of the devil, to recall Chemnitz—while Paul teaches timeless truths about salvation. Lapide is flipping the formula. He reads Paul's discussion of works as addressing the historically specific problem of Judaizing Christians, who abounded in the first century, while James articulates timeless truths about the new law of Christ, a teaching that is integral to the gospel.

It is fascinating that while Lapide's reading of Paul is motivated by the doctrinal assumptions of Trent and not historical-critical methods, he ends up with results that largely correspond to the scholarly consensus about Paul that has emerged since Krister Stendhal's groundbreaking criticisms of standard Protestant interpretations. But that is beside the point. What concerns us is the charge that doctrine corrupts "objective" interpretation. This is

9. Cornelius à Lapide, *Commentaria in Scripturam Sacram, Tomus Vigesimus* (Paris, 1861), 133.

not the case for Lapide. The presumption that the Council of Trent teaches true doctrine certainly motivates his speculations about the *Sitz im Leben* for Paul's epistles. He is theorizing about historical context, not "proving" Tridentine doctrine with his exegesis.

———

The sample above is small. Nevertheless, Luther, Chemnitz, Calvin, and Lapide shed light on what actually happens when doctrinal commitments provide the horizon of truth for exegesis. Acknowledging the remarkable exegetical creativity triggered by Reformation debates about justification offers a useful corrective to our uninformed assumptions about the supposedly negative consequences of bringing doctrine into the house of interpretation. These Reformation-era readers did not prove their doctrinal assumptions by quoting specific texts. Proof-texting is a modern practice encouraged by the rationalist and scientistic ideologies that have flourished in recent centuries. When it comes to the doctrine of justification, proof-texting makes no sense. A canon that includes both James and Paul turns the doctrine into a problem that must be solved. Solutions can be pursued textually with reference to historical context (as in Luther, Chemnitz, and Lapide), or they can be pursued doctrinally with close analysis of key concepts (as in Calvin's distinction between the two meanings of faith).

These readers saturated their interpretations of Paul and James with historical observations, scholastic distinctions, and remarks about the original context of Scripture. They did so not out of a vague curiosity but out of a sense of urgency. How can one sustain true doctrine in light of apparent counter-testimonies in Scripture? To a large degree this saturation of exegesis with observations about history, morality, metaphysics, psychology, and every other discipline *is* Christian theology. To put the same point differently: Christian theology operates with a wide range of intellectual practices that provide historical judgments, conceptual distinctions, and textual nuance for faithful readers of the Bible, and it does so in order that they may be able to sustain doctrinally governed readings. Without doctrinal priorities, exegesis easily becomes one-dimensional and flat, often falling into the set patterns and tiresome routines of merely academic convention. This is one reason why older historical-critical interpreters are so interesting—they were invested in church teaching—while contemporary academic criticism often seems less vigorous and creative. The exceptions are feminist and other ideologically driven interpreters. They adhere to secular doctrines. This adherence motivates them to offer adventurous readings that bring the obscurity and diversity of Scripture into a coherent form under the governance of their overarching hypothesis about the central importance of patriarchy, colonialism, empire, or some fundamental power that they take to be the supreme governor of human affairs.

Secular or religious, orthodox or heterodox, doctrine provides the schematic drawing for organizing the mosaic of Scripture; it establishes a horizon of truth for interpretation. For centuries, Protestants and Catholics were divided over the doctrine of justification. Notwithstanding ecumenical statements, many think these traditions remain divided. But as the great figures we considered above demonstrate, they are united in what I have been calling their theological interpretation. Their doctrinal commitments spur them to develop histories of the canon, to analyze the concept of faith, and to nuance scriptural passages. And they do all this so that they can prove that Paul and James do not contradict each other. They adhere to the presumption of accordance—the fundamental Christian conviction that church doctrine and sound exegesis flow from the same always-flowing spring of divine revelation.

The conceits of modern critics are just that—conceits. They are not accurate accounts of premodern interpretation. Neither Luther nor Lapide is using Scripture as a proof text for doctrine. To evoke Saint Augustine's famous distinction between *use* and *enjoyment*, they are *using* their doctrinal commitments to frame their interpretations. The doctrine of justification (however understood) guides them as they try to solve the puzzle of Scripture. How can Paul and James say what they say without contradicting each other?[10] In Luther's and Lapide's exegesis, doctrine is not *in* the Bible. Rather, doctrine is what they need to take into account if they are to *enjoy* a glimpse of the handsome king to whom the Bible as a whole testifies. We would do well to imitate their practice, even if we dissent from their understandings of the doctrine of justification and pursue very different readings of Paul and James.

10. See Augustine, *De doctrina Christiana*, book 1. For an example of St. Augustine's own exegetical use of doctrine, see his brief digression into a verse of the Song of Songs in book 2, chapter 6.

5

IN THE BEGINNING

"IN THE BEGINNING GOD CREATED the heavens and the earth." This familiar and time-honored translation of the first verse of the Bible follows the Septuagint, the ancient Greek translation of the Old Testament that was widely used in Hellenistic Judaism and early Christianity.[1] As I've noted in previous chapters, "in the beginning" has important doctrinal implications. It evokes an absolute beginning that is explicit in the opening verse of the Gospel of John: "In the beginning was the Word." And the traditional translation of Genesis 1:1 dovetails quite nicely with the doctrine of creation out of nothing, an instance of accordance that I've used to illustrate the nature of theological exegesis. In this chapter, I want to enter more fully into the interplay of Scripture and doctrine, for the fruitful back-and-forth is richly evident in a theological reading of the opening verses of Genesis.

These days, Genesis 1:1 is often translated "In the beginning when God created" or "When God began to create." The sense of a beginning that is absolute and foundational is muted, even contradicted, and the close association of Genesis 1:1 with John 1:1 is obscured. Many biblical scholars regard these outcomes as

---

1. See RSV, NIV, NASB, and others.

desirable. Christian doctrine, we are told, impedes good biblical exegesis. We're better off with translations that deter readers who presume the interpretive fittingness of the Christian tradition.

But is it true that doctrines such as *creatio ex nihilo* are alien to good interpretation? It is important to realize that there is nothing in the Hebrew itself that can settle for us the proper sense of Genesis 1:1. Moreover, a word such as "beginning" has many shades of meaning. A point of departure can refer to a discrete moment in time: "The train began its trip at 7:25 p.m." Following this sense, the preference of contemporary translators for a more temporal and restricted role for "beginning" is certainly plausible. Yet a point of departure or beginning can also refer to the basis or rationale for something, its purpose or reason. A scientist might say, "The second law of thermodynamics is the foundation—the beginning—of my cosmology." Or he could say, "Professor Smith's class was the basis—the beginning—of my love of science." Professor Smith was not his first science teacher. Rather, he was the one who sparked a passion for scientific inquiry, and a spark does not occur only at a specific point in time; it can serve as an ongoing basis or origin.

The senses of "beginning" as source and origin are associated with the Greek term *archē*, which means a basis and foundation, as well as a starting point in time. From this word we get "archaeology," the study of a culture's material origins. *Archē* is used in the Septuagint to translate Genesis 1:1, and it is repeated in John 1:1. Of course, the sense of "beginning" conveyed in the notion of an origin or source rather than a first instance in time is not only a Greek idea. The Bible teaches, "The fear of the LORD is the beginning of wisdom" (Ps. 111:10). The claim is substantive, not temporal. Fear of the Lord is the foundation of the wise life, providing its basis or root.[2]

2. For a full development of the different possible senses of "beginning," see Origen's *Commentary on John* 1.16–22. For Origen's rejection of the merely temporal sense of "beginning" for understanding Gen. 1:1, see his *Homilies on Genesis* 1.1.

These observations about the different senses of "beginning" raise an interesting exegetical problem. The old translation, "in the beginning," brings to mind fairly traditional ideas of God as the eternal and self-sufficient deity whose creative act initiates time and brings forth all things. The new translations imply that God is a deity who at a certain point in time set about to form the world out of preexisting matter. Which, then, shall it be? Are we to cleave to the traditional translation and its close association with *creatio ex nihilo*? Or should we follow contemporary scholarly judgments?

―――

As I have noted, the Hebrew original offers no clear guidance. But I don't think we should regret the lack of easy answers. It matters a great deal how we read Genesis 1:1. The traditional interpretations, supported by the older translation rooted in the ancient Greek version of the Old Testament, play important roles in the doctrine of creation (as well as in trinitarian theology). This combination of uncertainty and consequence creates interpretive pressure. We must rouse ourselves to think more deeply about the opening chapter of Genesis. And this is a good outcome. The greatest impediment to reading the Bible well in our time is not the temptation of fundamentalism. Our problems are disinterest and complacency, perennial problems made worse by the modern conceit that we're beneficiaries of moral and spiritual progress that put us in a position superior to the Bible and its earlier readers.

So let's entertain the pressure that doctrinal commitments put on biblical interpretation. In order to take the first step toward a larger view, I want to turn to Rashi, the great eleventh-century Jewish commentator. He makes brief but fecund observations that help us understand the exegetical richness of classical doctrine.

In his commentary on Genesis, Rashi notes an earlier rabbinic opinion. It holds that the Pentateuch should have begun with

Exodus 12:2 and not Genesis 1:1. This opinion is based on the traditional rabbinic view that Exodus 12:2 expresses the first commandment that God gives to Israel, and in that sense inaugurates the giving of the Torah at Sinai. By saying that the Bible ought to have begun at this juncture, the rabbis were conveying an important theological judgment: God creates for the sake of the Torah. But the rabbis are doing more than hanging a theological idea on a biblical verse. If we turn to Exodus 12:2, we see that the literal sense of that verse echoes Genesis 1:1: "This month shall be for you the beginning of months." God immediately reiterates: "It shall be the first month of the year for you." If we look at the larger context, we see that the material that follows Exodus 12:2 concerns preparations for the Passover, the narrow gate through which the descendants of Abraham must pass in order to enter into the fullness of God's promise.

Given this material, the plain sense of Exodus 12:2 is that the Passover festival is the "beginning" of Judaism's lunar calendar. But it falls in the month of Nisan, a springtime month, while Rosh Hashanah, the Jewish New Year, inaugurates Tishri, a month in the fall. How, then, are we to read God's declaration that Nisan should be the first month, the year's "beginning"? The apparent contradiction is resolved if we interpret "beginning" as basis, purpose, or rationale. The Passover and subsequent revelation on Mount Sinai function as the *archē* of creation. God's plan for the people of Israel, Rashi implies, is the most elementary and fundamental aspect of creation. Just as the fear of the Lord is the beginning of wisdom, so the giving of the law is the beginning in which and for which God creates. As Karl Barth puts it, covenant is the inner basis of creation.[3]

The ancient Hebrew text of the Old Testament does not include vowels. They were added in the Masoretic version, which scholars

---

3. See Karl Barth, *Church Dogmatics* III/1, *The Doctrine of Creation, Part 1*, trans. G. W. Bromiley, ed. T. F. Torrance (Edinburgh: T&T Clark, 1958), 43–44.

believe was developed sometime after the seventh century. This later version of Genesis supports the contemporary translations and their alternatives to "in the beginning." Yet Rashi, who was intimately familiar with the Masoretic version, reads Genesis differently. His citation of the old opinion that the Bible ought to have begun with Exodus 12:2 supports the Septuagint's translation of the first verse. The Torah is the "beginning," which means that "in the beginning"—in and for the sake of the Torah—God created.

It is interesting to note that the traditional rabbinic opinion that God starts with the Torah adopts the same sense of "beginning" as does the prologue to the Gospel of John. John 1:1, like Exodus 12:2, employs the crucial word "beginning." The opening verses of the Gospel of John indicate that God created in and for the sake of the incarnation of the Word. It is not that Rashi or any other Jewish commentator agrees that Christ, the incarnate Word, is the *archē* of creation, its inner basis. Rather, the traditional opinion about Exodus 12:2 that Rashi cites and the wording of the first verse of the Gospel of John share a common theological judgment. The divine project, whether spelled out in terms of Torah or Christ, is the "beginning" out of which and for which God creates.[4]

At this point, I can hear the objections. Formulations such as "When God began to create" or "In the beginning when God created" win support from modern scholars at least in part because they deem that traditional theological loyalties have for too long overdetermined our reading of Scripture. This concern becomes particularly acute when biblical scholars see the New Testament functioning as the lens through which we read the Old Testament. I do not want to gainsay the contemporary desire to

---

4. Rashi does not explicate this priority in metaphysical terms. Instead, as his comment on Gen. 1:1 continues, he observes the way in which creation occurs for the sake of the moral cogency of the covenant. The people of Israel rightly claim the land because it was created for them—that is to say, for the sake of the covenant—"in the beginning."

recover the integrity of the distinctive voices of the diverse books of the Bible. Yet I worry that modern assumptions about biblical interpretation suffer from "presentism." Today's scholars are often blind to the wealth of reasons in favor of traditional readings.

As I have argued in earlier chapters, exegetical judgments do not emerge *ex nihilo*, achieve communal authority, and then impose themselves on the interpretive imaginations of traditional readers of the Bible. Traditional readers turn to doctrine because they find its application to be exegetically fruitful. This fruitfulness is not surprising, for the doctrines were developed to aid the work of scriptural interpretation. Rashi does not repeat the older opinion about Exodus 12:2 because he is a "traditionalist." He is signaling a foundational theological judgment about the relation of creation and redemption that finds support throughout Scripture. The same can be said of John 1:1. Using the translation "in the beginning" and affirming its connotations of *creatio ex nihilo* is the most plausible way to interpret Genesis 1:1 because it supports a full-scale reading of Scripture as a whole.

———

Let's begin with the larger sweep of the first chapter of Genesis. The days of creation move forward in a temporal sequence, culminating in the seventh day, the Sabbath. But in spite of this apparent focus on *when* things happen, the dominant rhetorical note of the first chapter of Genesis concerns *how* God creates. The days are punctuated with a common refrain: "And God said." This rhetorical pattern encourages us to paraphrase the first verse of Genesis in the following way: "In the beginning—in what God said, which is to say, in his Word—God created the heavens and the earth." The author of the Gospel of John is writing with the grain of Genesis.

A substantive reading of "beginning" finds additional textual support. Many ancient commentators saw an obvious difficulty standing in the way of a straightforward, temporal reading of "in the beginning." One puzzle of the first chapter of Genesis is that the sun, moon, and stars are created on the fourth day. How, then, can there be a "first day" when the sun does not exist? What marks the difference between day and night? And even if the sun exists, at any moment half of the earth is in darkness while the other half is bathed in light. We cannot think of the earth as a whole (to say nothing of the larger universe) as existing in a comprehensive state of "day" or "night." In view of these difficulties, Augustine worried that a strictly temporal reading of the creation account in Genesis would entangle us in countless difficulties. "I fear," he says, "that I will be laughed at by those who have scientific knowledge of these matters and by those who recognize the facts of the case."[5]

There are still further reasons to sustain the traditional reading and translation. In this case, we can draw on insights from modern biblical scholarship. In the terminology of modern biblical study, the first chapter of Genesis reflects the interests and worldview of P (the Priestly writer), while the second chapter stems from J (the Yahwist). I find this speculation about the sources of material in Genesis to be convincing. It encourages us to give close attention to the place of the first creation account within the larger body of Priestly writings. As a historian, therefore, the first and most important thing to say about the entire account of creation that opens Genesis is that it stems from a tradition that wishes to place temple and sacrifice at the center of our perceptions of the deepest logic and purpose of reality. In other words, the divine plan of temple and sacrifice is the *archē* of the Priestly writer's view of creation. In this regard, the results of modern historical-critical study encourage us to say, "In the beginning was the temple cult and its ideological outworkings." This conclusion runs counter to

5. Augustine, *The Literal Meaning of Genesis* 1.10, in *On Genesis*, trans. Edmund Hill, The Works of Saint Augustine I/13 (Hyde Park, NY: New City, 2002), 178. See also *City of God* 11.7.

the contemporary preference for a thin, temporally focused reading of the first verse. It is another mark in favor of the traditional translation.[6]

I have itemized some textual reasons in support of "In the beginning." Now I want to broaden my argument, not only because I think the reasons are compelling but also because we need to be clear-minded about the full scope of interpretation. Theological readers are *theo-logical* because they want to read Scripture in such a way as to sustain a coherent view of God's plan and purpose. Sustaining a coherent view involves complex and sometimes opaque layers of argument. In this instance, I identify three advantages that speak in favor of the traditional translation. An interpretation of beginning guided by the doctrine of creation out of nothing (1) helps us avoid a false conflict between creation and science, (2) facilitates a faithful engagement of faith with reason, and (3) maximizes the spiritual fruitfulness of our interpretive concerns.

Modern cosmology is concerned with the movements of matter and energy that have brought about reality as we know it. This investigation suggests the sense of "beginning" understood as temporal sequence.[7] For this reason, the interpretation of "beginning" in a fuller sense—as reality's ultimate source or basis—need not directly and primarily concern itself with modern cosmology. A modern scientist may argue, as does Richard Dawkins, that

6. For further historical-critical reasons along these lines, see Gerhard von Rad's extensive analysis of the redacted form of the Hexateuch. Von Rad argues that the larger canonical context of Gen. 1 and 2 encourages an interpretation of "beginning" that anticipates God's acts of deliverance. "Israel looked back in faith from her own election to creation, and from there drew a line to herself from the outermost limit of the protological to the center of the soteriological" (*Genesis: A Commentary*, trans. John H. Marks [Philadelphia: Westminster, 1974], 46). Here, von Rad agrees with the ancient rabbis, whom Rashi cites in his comment on Gen. 1:1.

7. See, for example, Steven Weinberg, *The First Three Minutes: A Modern View of the Origin of the Universe* (New York: Basic Books, 1977).

there is no intent or purpose undergirding the world.[8] But such a pronouncement reflects a philosophical judgment, not a scientific one. Dawkins is assuming that what modern science can or cannot determine is coextensive with what is or is not the case. This is an assertion, not a scientific postulate. The claim that the universe has no meaning or purpose is not part of scientific cosmology. Thus, a substantive reading of "beginning" in Genesis 1:1 allows the Christian interpreter to embrace modern science while clarifying a properly Christian rejection of modern scientism.[9]

The second advantage concerns the focus of our interpretive activity. If we adopt a reading of the first verse of Genesis that follows the direction of Exodus 12:2 and its use of "beginning" as basis or purpose, then our interpretive questions are forthright and bring us directly to a theological question that ought to concern any Christian (and Jew): What *is* God's plan "in the beginning"?

The writers of the New Testament were well aware of the central importance of this question. The author of the Gospel of John was not the only one to frame creation in terms of the divine plan. As Saint Paul writes, "There is one God, the Father, from whom are all things and for whom we exist, and one Lord, Jesus Christ, through whom are all things and through whom we exist" (1 Cor. 8:6). Paul's formulation is an exposition of Genesis 1:1 that goes like this: In (through) the beginning (Christ), God, the Father, created heaven and earth.

Governed by this account of creation, Paul and the subsequent Christian tradition give priority to revelation in Christ in a way that harmonizes faith with reason. Knowing the Lord Jesus is crucial to knowing the beginning in which and out of which all things come to be. As Augustine exhorts, "Mark this fabric of the world.

8. See Richard Dawkins, *The Blind Watchmaker* (New York: Penguin, 1990). Modernist protology would seem to be precisely the wandering away in "meaningless talk" that St. Paul warns against (1 Tim. 1:6).

9. For a clear explanation of the import of modern cosmology and its relationship to classical doctrines of creation, see Stephen M. Barr, *Modern Physics and Ancient Faith* (Notre Dame, IN: University of Notre Dame Press, 2003).

View what was made by the Word, and then you will understand
what is the nature of the world."[10] Christ is the master plan; he
is the "beloved Son" who is the "firstborn of all creation"; Christ
is the beginning, "for in him all things . . . were created" (Col.
1:13–16). His saving death was planned "before the foundation
of the world" (1 Pet. 1:20). The Lord is "the bright morning star"
(Rev. 22:16) by which the faithful take their bearings, and "in [him]
are hidden all the treasures of wisdom and knowledge" (Col. 2:3).

In each of these passages from the New Testament, the world
does not only have a beginning in time; it has a beginning in the
divine plan, the Word. With this knowledge, we can return to the
relation of science with religion, this time with a theological affirmation of their proper and fruitful mutual support. Accurate
knowledge of reality (what used to be called natural philosophy)
guides us toward the originating Word. Recall Augustine: "Mark
the fabric of this world." Reason can prepare us for faith. And the
street goes both ways. Theology orients our minds to the truth of
all things. Faith brings us to an ever more intimate union with the
archē of creation, and thus faith perfects reason.

The third benefit that flows from adopting "in the beginning"
as our reading of the opening verse of Genesis bears directly on a
central problem in Christian theology, the relation between nature
and grace. The absolute sense of "beginning" stipulated by the
doctrine of *creatio ex nihilo* allows for a Christ-centered reading
of God's creation. This in turn helps explain the perplexing double
affirmation that characterizes apostolic Christianity. On the one
hand, everything is good; on the other hand, everything must
change. To put the matter more concretely, not only are human
creatures finite and exist as natural aspects of the created order;

10. Augustine, *Tractates on the Gospel according to Saint John* 1.9 (https://www
.newadvent.org/fathers/1701001.htm). The theological judgment is by no means
merely antique. See Robert W. Jenson, *Systematic Theology*, vol. 2 (New York: Oxford University Press, 1999): "The story told in the Gospels states the meaning of
creation" (27).

they are also chosen and called to fellowship with God. As the story of Genesis moves forward, Abraham must leave home. He is called to transcend the natural bonds of filial love and forsake the safety of his clan. This leave-taking is intensified in Christian discipleship. Consider the demands of the Sermon on the Mount! The ordinary stuff of life—our bodies, our desires, our loyalties, our identities as social creatures—all this is called beyond what seems natural and normal. We are created, yes, but our divinely ordained destiny is to live as adopted children of God.

The puzzle of the relation of nature and grace is fundamental. As I have argued elsewhere, the apparent contradiction between the goodness of creation and the necessity of redemption is highly relevant to modern doubts about the truth of the gospel.[11] How can God call creation "very good" and then turn around and continue to act upon it for the sake of pushing the human creature toward an even higher goal? How can the human body be good and God nonetheless require of Abraham circumcision for the sake of covenant? How can we harmonize the divine directive "Be fruitful and multiply" with the Pauline exhortation to prefer the celibate life?

These difficulties are resolved if we adopt an absolute sense of "beginning" rather than a narrowly temporal one suggested by the translation "When God began to create." Christ is the master plan of all creation—its beginning. Thus, his call to discipleship leads toward a fulfillment of nature rather than its effacement or denial. As Athanasius observes, "There is thus no inconsistency between creation and salvation for the One Father has employed the same Agent for both works, effecting the salvation of the world through the same Word Who made it in the beginning."[12] In following

11. See R. R. Reno, "Redemption and Ethics," in *The Oxford Handbook of Theological Ethics*, ed. Gilbert Meilaender and William Werpehowski (New York: Oxford University Press, 2007), 25–40.
12. Athanasius, *On the Incarnation* 1, trans. Penelope Lawson (http://www.romans45.org/history/ath-inc.htm#ch_1).

Christ toward an end that is supernatural, we will not (to echo Nietzsche) vivisect our fragile, finite, natural lives. That which is created shall not be defeated or destroyed; it will "be swallowed up by life" (2 Cor. 5:4). In the words of T. S. Eliot, "And the end of all our exploring / Will be to arrive where we started / And know the place for the first time."[13]

The second verse of Genesis seems fairly clear: "The earth was without form and void, and darkness was upon the face of the deep; and the Spirit of God was moving over the face of the waters" (RSV). But for traditional readers of Genesis, a commitment to *creatio ex nihilo* makes these lines very troublesome. Instead of speaking all reality into existence, God seems to tame and form a preexisting chaos, acting upon a primal, watery substance. Modern biblical scholars have detailed connections between this verse and the Babylonian creation myth, Enuma Elish. The parallel crops up in a number of different places in the Old Testament.[14] But modern scholars are by no means the first to notice that the plain sense of Genesis 1:2 suggests creation out of preexisting, primal substance rather than creation out of nothing. As Augustine reports in his commentary on Genesis, "The heretics [he is referring to Manichaeans] who reject the Old Testament are in the habit of pointing the finger at this passage and saying, 'How can God have made heaven and earth in the beginning, if the earth was already there?'"[15]

The plain sense may encourage the heretics. But as Augustine points out, they face a roadblock. The doctrine of *creatio ex nihilo*

13. T. S. Eliot, "Little Gidding," in *Four Quartets* (New York: Harcourt, Brace, 1943), 59.

14. See Jon D. Levenson, *Creation and the Persistence of Evil* (San Francisco: Harper & Row, 1988).

15. Augustine, *Unfinished Literal Commentary on Genesis* 4, in *On Genesis*, trans. Edmund Hill, The Works of Saint Augustine I/13 (Hyde Park, NY: New City, 2002), 129.

bars the way. However we might read this verse and its evocation of an enigmatic formless void and watery chaos, Augustine observes, "we must believe that God is the Maker and Creator of all things."[16] The Christian reader who presumes the authority of classical doctrine cannot adopt an interpretation that allows for a preexistent formless void, a mysterious deep, a primal water. Such concessions contradict the doctrine of creation out of nothing.

Modern readers recoil at the notion that doctrine should be relevant to scriptural interpretation. Aren't we supposed to adopt a critically responsible approach to the Bible? And if we do, we must acknowledge that, aside from 2 Maccabees 7:28, the (Catholic) Bible does not explicitly teach creation out of nothing. It would seem, then, that the conflict between *creatio ex nihilo* and the plain sense of Genesis 1:2 presents us with a classic case of preconceived theological ideas subverting the literal meaning of the Bible. A rigid system of doctrine is being imposed upon Scripture and silencing its own voice. "It is one thing to respect the traditional views and interpretations of the Bible," we easily find ourselves insisting, "but we must be sure not to lose touch with what the text actually says."

As I've noted before, I sympathize with the impulse to defend the Scriptures against simpleminded absorption into preconceived doctrinal systems. A reading of Scripture that ignores or distorts the text makes a mockery of our commitment to the Bible as the Word of God. But we need to relax for a moment. Doctrines such as *creatio ex nihilo* became authoritative because Christian (and Jewish) readers have found them to be helpful guides to a coherent overall reading of Scripture. If we bracket the literal sense of the second verse of Genesis for a moment, we can see how the doctrine of *creatio ex nihilo* (1) maximizes the plain sense of the Scriptures, (2) supports a metaphysical framework for coherent affirmation of scriptural claims about God, and (3) provides a

16. Augustine, *Unfinished Literal Commentary on Genesis* 4.

spiritual, soteriological focus for biblical interpretation as a whole. I've noted the advantages of this in chapters 1 and 2. I want to go into more detail here.

——

Let's begin with the overall scriptural context. The Old Testament campaign against idolatry consistently implies the doctrine of creation out of nothing. Idols are not weak, ineffective, or inadequate; they are empty and lifeless. Those who set up idols in violation of God's commands "are nothing; their images are empty wind" (Isa. 41:29). "The makers of idols go into confusion" (45:16). Idol worship is, of course, disastrous for Israel, but the images themselves do not possess evil powers. Idols are "like scarecrows," and "they cannot do evil, nor is it in them to do good" (Jer. 10:5).

The New Testament carries forward the same view. Idols are lifeless and powerless. Paul explains the futility of idols by appealing to God's creative uniqueness (see Acts 14:15; 17:24), which is another way of stating the doctrine of creation out of nothing. Paul is indifferent to concerns that pagan meat sacrifices might be infected by a hidden, shameful potency (see 1 Cor. 8). Idols are not malignantly powerful; they are empty and vacant. The danger is not that idols will bewitch us because of their internal, semi-divine substance. They transfix because *we* will fill their vacancy with the noisy gongs and clanging cymbals of empty prophecy and pseudo-mystery (1 Cor. 13:1).

Given this biblical consensus about idols, it is not surprising that themes of idolatry and loyalty set the stage for the direct affirmation of *creatio ex nihilo* in 2 Maccabees 7:28.[17] By requiring us to adopt a parsimonious metaphysical view, the doctrine

17. For a patristic analysis of idolatry that presumes *creatio ex nihilo*, see Athanasius, *Contra Gentes* 8. For a contemporary study of idolatry that emphasizes the importance of the ontological parsimony (though cast in modern phenomenological terms), see Jean-Luc Marion, *The Idol and Distance*, trans. Thomas A. Carlson (New York: Fordham University Press, 2001).

of creation out of nothing supports the main lines of the biblical analysis of idolatry. There is nothing (*nihil*) other than the one true God and all the things that are the work of his hand. There are no intervening, eternal, and semi-divine powers or realities. Idolatry is thus not a metaphysical mistake or miscalculation. Its error does not rest in loyalty to a primeval, chaotic, and semi-divine substance that cannot measure up to the power and glory of the Lord. Idolatry makes a spiritual mistake; it implicates us in the worship of *nihil*, nothingness. Idols seduce us and guide us toward a devotion to lifelessness, which is the antithesis of the abundance of life promised in the covenant (see, for example, Deut. 30:19). Moses urges the Israelites to choose life—the opposite of the nihilism of idolatry.

The ontological parsimony entailed by the doctrine of creation out of nothing does more than undergird the Bible's warnings about idolatry. It also helps biblical readers manage the apparent conflict between two kinds of biblical claims about God. On the one hand, we read declarations of God's transcendence. "Even heaven and the highest heaven cannot contain you" (1 Kings 8:27). God is wholly other and cannot be framed within the finite world. On the other hand, we read of God's actions in the world. He commands and speaks, and in places such as Genesis 17:1, God "appears." Which shall it be? Is God without or within? Is God wholly other or is he present as the author of the unfolding drama of salvation?

These questions concern more than an intra-scriptural tension. They reflect contemporary intuitions about the universality of truth and the particularity of cultures. The bumper-sticker declaration "My God is too big for any one religion" expresses the conviction that one must be loyal to 1 Kings 8:27 to the exclusion of Genesis 17:1. The slogan asks us to affirm the universal deity in contradiction to the Lord who elects a particular nation, the twelve tribes of Israel. The contrastive choice between universality and particularity is all the more dramatic in classical Christology.

Divine transcendence would seem utterly inconsistent with the incarnation of the Second Person of the Trinity in the person of Jesus of Nazareth.

Creatio ex nihilo shows that this contrastive choice between transcendence and presence rests on a false dichotomy. The doctrine teaches that, prior to creation, God is in relation to absolutely nothing other than himself. There exists no eternal substance against which God is defined as divine. In this way, the doctrine of creation out of nothing leads us to conceive of God's transcendence in terms of uniqueness rather than in terms of difference from, supremacy to, or primacy over something else. As Exodus 3:14 states, God is who he is simply because he is who he is, and not because he is not something else. Exodus 3:15 strikes the same metaphysical note in a different key. God's revealed name, YHWH, is more fundamental than contrastive terms such as the Eternal or the Almighty.[18]

The fact that *creatio ex nihilo* formulates God's transcendence in terms of uniqueness rather than supremacy or difference means that the transcendence of God is consistent with his presence in finite reality. When God comes to those whom he loves, he leaves nothing behind. There is no divine reality other than the singular Lord, and therefore he neither betrays nor contradicts his divinity by drawing near. Someone formed by traditional doctrine need not feel compelled to choose between the universal God of the philosophers and the Lord who acts in space and time.[19] Nor does the reader of the Gospels need to parse divinity and humanity in the words and deeds of the one person Jesus Christ.[20] Here, the central importance of the doctrine of creation out of nothing for

18..For this reason, the use of the divine name by the J material of Genesis involves an implicit doctrine of creation that is every bit as theocentric as the P material in Gen. 1.

19. On this point and with the same argument, see St. Thomas, *Summa Theologiae* I.13.7.resp.

20. See Origen, *Contra Celsum* 4.5. For a helpful discussion of the way in which *creatio ex nihilo* provides crucial background for christological doctrine, see Robert

our reading of Genesis 1:2 should be plain, as it was for Saint Augustine. Any contradiction of *creatio ex nihilo* and its ontological parsimony will undermine the capacity of scriptural readers to interpret the Lord God of Israel as the universal deity. Without this doctrine, Nicene doctrine becomes incoherent.[21]

At this juncture, I must pause to express my exasperation with modern, anti-dogmatic sensibilities. Rejecting the exegetical authority of the doctrine of creation out of nothing does not preserve the integrity of the biblical text. If we set aside *creatio ex nihilo*, then perhaps we can become more intimate with a scholarly construct called "ancient Israelite religion." But that construct is occult, the product of scholarly speculation. And it is inconsequential, because it is not a living option for us. I've come to see that scholars find notions such as ancient Israelite religion easy to believe because they are largely irrelevant to our most important convictions about life, morality, and faith. But this irrelevance comes at a cost. If we set aside the doctrine of creation out of nothing, our approach to the Bible as a whole slides toward incoherence, and our talk about God becomes vaguely metaphorical at best. *Creatio ex nihilo* was developed to avoid this incoherence and theological flabbiness.

The third and final reason to affirm *creatio ex nihilo* is rooted in the gospel itself. The doctrine demands christological maximalism.[22] Irenaeus based his rejection of Gnostic accounts of Jesus's role as Savior on a complex refutation of the Gnostic doctrine of creation.[23] Gnostics saw the created world as a product of cosmic evolution. This process generates layers of spiritual or supernatural

---

Sokolowski, *The God of Faith and Reason: Foundations of Christian Theology* (Washington, DC: Catholic University of America Press, 1982), 31–40.

21. For a discussion of the theologically paralyzing consequences of placing God within a well-furnished metaphysical system, see William C. Placher, *The Domestication of Transcendence: How Modern Thinking about God Went Wrong* (Louisville: Westminster John Knox, 1996).

22. I take the term "christological maximalism" from George A. Lindbeck. See *The Nature of Doctrine: Religion and Theology in a Postliberal Age* (Philadelphia: Westminster, 1984), 92–96.

23. Irenaeus, *Against Heresies* 1.

reality that flow from the deity. With this ontological ladder at
their disposal—the very opposite of parsimony—Gnostics could
avoid the counterintuitive claim that Jesus is God incarnate. Jesus
has a role on the ladder of being. He is above us in ontological
significance, offering us a hand up, as it were, pulling us toward
consummation with the One. Irenaeus strenuously rejected the
notion of a semi-divine mediator, and his reasoning adds up to a
case for the doctrine of creation out of nothing. The doctrine's
ontological parsimony requires us to make a binary choice: Jesus is
either a mere human being, like you and me, or he is God incarnate.

The analysis Irenaeus provides draws upon the broad *sola gratia* emphasis of the New Testament's reading of the Old. Saint
Paul's analysis of Abraham's justification and the larger project
of divine blessing rejects the notion that there are any mediating
realities between God and creation. Upon what might Abraham
rely other than God? He alone "gives life to the dead and calls
into existence the things that do not exist" (Rom. 4:17). All other
powers are "as good as dead" (4:19), says Paul, using terms that
echo the Old Testament's polemic against idolatry. We must rely
on God alone, for we cannot rely on worldly powers, especially not
on our own willpower. In these affirmations of salvation by grace
alone, the ontological parsimony entailed by *creatio ex nihilo*
manifests its soteriological significance. It resists the temptation
to rely on idols (or on our own works), pressing us toward Christ
alone as the power of salvation.[24]

There are further warrants supporting the authority of the doctrine of creation out of nothing over our interpretation of Genesis

24. The same *sola gratia* conclusion characterizes Jewish thought about the relation between worldly powers and divinely given law. See Joseph Soloveitchik's rejection
of *Homo religiosus* and the perennial urge to climb up the Great Chain of Being in
Halakhic Man (Philadelphia: Jewish Publication Society, 1983). "*Homo religiosus*
ascends to God," Soloveitchik writes. "God, however, descends to halakhic man" (45).

1:2. But my goal has not been to provide an exhaustive account. Rather, I have tried to show that doctrinal governance of scriptural interpretation is not a simpleminded submission to nonbiblical authority. The substance of traditional doctrines arises from and supports an array of complex, multilayered exegetical judgments that operate across the biblical text as a whole.

Christian readers rarely felt the need to make explicit the extensive exegetical rationales for their translations and doctrines. They trusted in the scriptural integrity of the Christian tradition as a whole. One of the most important objectives of modern critical scholarship has been to undermine this trust. More than one hundred years ago, the widely influential Old Testament scholar C. A. Briggs expressed this modern, anti-traditional sentiment: "Holy Scripture, as given by holy prophets, lies buried beneath the rubbish of centuries." "The valleys of biblical truth," Briggs continues, "have been filled up with the debris of human dogmas, ecclesiastical institutions, liturgical formulas, priestly ceremonies, and casuistic practices." According to Briggs and many other modern biblical scholars, we must get rid of the influence of centuries of interpretation "in order to recover the real Bible." We need to toss out tradition—for the sake of the gospel.

I do not want to end by pointing out that, in the mentality of Briggs and countless other modern biblical scholars, the Protestant *sola scriptura* has degenerated into a sterile modernism. Nor do I want to play the postmodern critic by observing that it is naive to imagine that we can dig down to the "real Bible," untainted by interpretation.[25] These criticisms have been pressed by others, but to little effect. The anti-dogmatic mentality of contemporary biblical study continues to perpetuate implausible methodological

25. For just these observations, see James L. Kugel, "The Bible in the University," in *The Hebrew Bible and Its Interpreters*, ed. William Henry Propp, Baruch Halpern, and David Noel Freedman (Winona Lake, IN: Eisenbrauns, 1990), 143–65. It was Kugel who drew my attention to Briggs, and from Kugel's book I have drawn the quotes above.

assumptions. Instead, I want to make a more straightforward observation. I hope this analysis of the opening verses of Genesis,
which I have undertaken a number of times in the volume, has
planted the suspicion in the minds of readers that traditional
doctrines are not extrinsic to interpretation. They do not overlay
the Bible as a suffocating blanket of prejudice. On the contrary,
traditions of translation and doctrine—as well as our traditions
of liturgy, prayer, and spiritual discipline—are deeply exegetical
in origin and consequence.

When modern exegetes ignore the resources of our tradition,
they often reinvent the interpretive wheel. Failing to draw on the
collective intelligence of faithful readers throughout the centuries,
their reinvented wheels often wobble and fail. To put the situation
in terms familiar to generations of seminary students, modern
biblical study does not preach. By my lights, the problem is not
modern historical consciousness. Nor is it the critical cast of mind,
which is well represented in the church fathers, the medieval Scho-
lastics, and the Reformers. Our problem arises from the impover-
ishment of our biblical interpretation by the anti-traditionalism
expressed by Briggs and implicitly endorsed by most modern biblical scholars. Without the guidance of the church's long experience
of reading the Bible, we end up with isolated, disjointed pieces
of Scripture surrounded by sophisticated reconstructions of their
historical contexts. Those reconstructions can be persuasive, even
fruitful for the church's ongoing tradition of reading. But for the
most part, we must rely on crude generalizations or vague theological gestures to link these disjointed pieces with the other parts
of the Bible, or with faithful Christian practice.[26]

We need to stop trying to reinvent scriptural interpretation.
We must avoid the illusion that our spiritually crippled age can
use its increasingly old and tired "critical methods" to recover

26. See my analysis of the failed exegetical strategies of modernity, "Biblical
Theology and Theological Exegesis," in *Out of Egypt: Biblical Theology and Biblical
Interpretation*, ed. Craig Bartholomew et al. (London: Paternoster, 2004), 385–408.

the "real Bible." Our inherited traditions need always to be tested and corrected by exegetical reflection. We certainly can include modern historical scholarship in this process. New studies of Paul in recent decades have made an important contribution to our understanding of the doctrine of justification, for example, as I noted in the previous chapter. But let us acknowledge that our inherited traditions are intrinsically and richly exegetical. They seek to answer the most difficult and central exegetical question of all: How can the Bible as a whole be read as the Word of God? Every generation faces this question, including our own. Our time is different in this regard, however. We seek to discern what God is saying to us in Scripture in a moral, spiritual, and intellectual culture that is increasingly hostile. Which is why it is foolish for us to ignore our dogmatic, ecclesiastical, liturgical, and spiritual traditions. When we take up and read the Bible, we need them now more than ever.

6

THAT THEY ALL MAY BE ONE

FOR MORE THAN A CENTURY, the seventeenth chapter of the Gospel of John has provided a powerful scriptural warrant for the ecumenical movement. Jesus's prayer to the Father in verse 21— "that they all may be one"[1]—echoes through many ecumenical documents, from Faith and Order statements in the early twentieth century, to the Second Vatican Council's Decree on Ecumenism, to contemporary calls for Christian unity. But in my view, modern ecumenical uses of John 17 tend to be flat-footed. "That they all may be one" too often functions as a stand-alone proof text. I propose, therefore, that we enrich our ecumenical imaginations with a more patient, more extensive, and more theological reading of this famous passage.

John 17 brings Jesus's so-called Farewell Discourse to a close. The discourse begins with chapter 13. The Passover festival is at hand; Jesus's hour has come. Jesus washes the feet of his disciples and prophesies his betrayal. After Judas departs, Jesus pronounces himself glorified, and he gives his disciples a new commandment: "That you love one another. Just as I have loved you, you also should love one another. By this everyone will know that you are

---

1. This traditional translation appears in the King James Version (KJV) and others.

my disciples, if you have love for one another" (John 13:34–35). This new commandment of love serves as the leitmotif for the Farewell Discourse. Love seeks union with the beloved. Love wishes to abide in the beloved, to be at-one with the beloved. The main thrust of the Farewell Discourse is therefore to be found in Jesus's instructions to his disciples about how they can be with him, even as he goes away; be at-one, even as he departs. The answer is found in love, for love transcends separation and distance.

How can this be so? Immediately before issuing his new commandment, Jesus has announced something strange and paradoxical. The one who loves his friends is going away. He is separating himself from his disciples: "Where I am going, you cannot come" (John 13:33). Peter doesn't like this idea at all. He understands that love seeks to be with the beloved, and therefore he wishes to continue to be at-one with Jesus. So he announces there's no place he won't go with Jesus. He'll even go to the point of death, if that's what it takes to remain in union with his teacher. But Jesus tells Peter, no, dear friend, you won't go with me. Quite the contrary, you'll run the other direction, denying me three times.

It is this tension—a love that wishes to draw near and a Savior who is going away—that characterizes the Farewell Discourse as a whole and provides the background for Jesus's extended prayer in John 17. On the one hand, we are to love as he has loved, which means drawing close to him and to one another. We are to abide in him and, by imitating his love, to abide in the fellowship of the disciples. And yet, it seems we can't do this because he is going somewhere we cannot go. That "somewhere" is left deliberately vague in these passages. The Farewell Discourse is conveyed in "figures" (John 16:25). But one doesn't need an advanced degree in theology to spell out why Jesus is going somewhere we can't. Jesus is divine. He is the one who was with the Father "from the beginning." But we are finite creatures. There is an infinite metaphysical distance between divinity and humanity, between Creator and creature. We are also sinners enclosed in upon ourselves, largely incapable of going any place that involves sacrificing our self-love. By contrast, Jesus is spotless and without sin. He is able to give of himself without reserve. We are captive to sin, while he is free in love.

But Jesus does not launch into theological digressions to explain why Peter (and by implication all of us) cannot go with him. Instead, he wishes to reassure: "Do not let your hearts be troubled." There is a spiritual way of "going with" Jesus: "Believe in God, believe also in me" (John 14:1). This "going with" in faith constitutes one of the main teachings of the Farewell Discourse. It is the way of atonement. We can be at-one with Christ if we believe.

After Jesus addresses Peter, it is telling that the same "Where I am going, you cannot come" and "Do not let your hearts be troubled" sequence of distance and enduring intimacy is repeated immediately with Thomas. Jesus tells his disciples, "In my Father's house there are many dwelling places" (John 14:2). In essence, he's reassuring them that, although he must go away, he will return and bring them to the Father to dwell with him. He is leaving, yes, but for the sake of a future, deeper, permanent unity—an at-oneness in love.

Thomas, like Peter, understands the imperative of love. He seeks to be united to him whom he loves. He is not satisfied with waiting for Jesus to return. He is eager to get going right away. He wants to be reunited with Jesus as soon as possible. So Thomas presses him: "How can we know the way?" (John 14:5). Again, Jesus teaches that, paradoxically, we can go with him even as he goes where we cannot follow. He states, "I am the way, and the truth, and the life" (14:6). We can abide in him by *knowing* him, a fundamental biblical word that connotes union with and participation in that which we know. We can remain with him in faith, abide in him, even as he goes where we cannot go. And in knowing him we know the Father. Put in Saint Paul's terms, faith is the spirit of adoption that conforms us to the image of the incarnate Son (see Rom. 8).

The tension between distance and intimacy gets recapitulated yet again, this time by Philip, and the lesson that faith unites us with Christ even as he goes where we cannot is repeated. Philip shifts the key. Instead of the paschal "going to the cross" that echoes in Peter's insistence that he will remain at-one with Jesus, or the eschatological pathway from present to future consummation that's in the background of Thomas's question, Philip expresses the desire to overcome the metaphysical distance between God and man: "Lord, show us the Father, and we will be satisfied" (John 14:8). But what could be farther from finite human flesh than the eternal Godhead? Jesus's answer is a rebuke. Perhaps the Lord tires of teaching the same lesson! Has Philip failed to understand? "Do you not believe that I am in the Father and the Father is in me?" (14:10). Faith in Jesus as the incarnate Son of God brings the Father to us, because in the Son we find the fullness of God. The Son is always at-one with the Father, and the Father with the Son. And so if we abide in the Son, we abide in the Father.

Not surprisingly, therefore, Jesus suddenly and significantly shifts the direction of his travel. He is no longer going away but instead is preparing to come closer still. On the day of his glorification on the cross, he will reveal himself as the one who lives—the One who is Life—and "on that day you will know that I am in my Father, and you in me, and I in you" (John 14:20). He is going away to the cross for the sake of coming to us (14:28). The distance of the cross, the distance none of the disciples can traverse, is for the sake of love's closer embrace. The atoning sacrifice that only Jesus can make—he is going where we cannot—is at the same time his coming to us in love, making us at-one with him.

To these words Jesus adds a crucial teaching. It reinforces his exhortation to believe in him. His love for his disciples (and for us) takes him away and to the cross: "No one has greater love than this, to lay down one's life for one's friends" (John 15:13). Therefore, if we abide in his love—if we keep his word and obey his command to love as he loves—we abide in him. In our conformity to his commandment, we actively participate in the reason for his departure from us. In love, we go with him in a spiritual sense, even as we're left behind. Yes, Jesus goes where we cannot go. He alone is our Savior. He alone can redeem the world. He alone is consubstantial with the Father. But we need not be troubled in our hearts. We need neither fear his departure nor weep over the infinite distance that separates human beings who live in sin from the almighty God who dwells in holiness. For if we love as he has commanded us to love, we abide in him. In love Jesus takes us where we cannot go.

As if to reinforce the point, in chapter 15 Jesus reiterates his new commandment: "This is my commandment, that you love one another as I have loved you" (John 15:12). He then restates the power of this commandment to forge an enduring union with him: "You are my friends if you do what I command you" (15:14). If we do as he does—love as he loves—we conform ourselves to him. In obedience to his commandment, we become Christlike and thus unite ourselves with him. In love we become a branch of the true vine.

Branches of the true vine bear good fruit, and we will be known by our fruit. It is at this point that Jesus warns his disciples that abiding in him will put them at odds with the world. The world hates him, and as he is in us and we are in him, we too are hated (John 15:18). "If they persecuted me, they will persecute you" (15:20). Jesus foresees that his disciples will accompany him to the cross—not on Good Friday, but eventually. Abiding in him, they will go with him, even as he goes before them.

The teaching here is subtle. Friendship with Christ overcomes the distance between God and man, between self-love and love of neighbor—but in so doing it opens up a new distance. This time the distance is between those who believe in Christ and those who live according to "the world." (In the Gospel of John, "the world"

does not mean creation but instead refers to the regime governed
by sin and death, which defines worldly existence after the fall.)
The distance between discipleship and worldliness will become
extreme: "They will put you out of the synagogues. Indeed, an
hour is coming when those who kill you will think that by doing
so they are offering worship to God" (John 16:2).

The prospect of friendship with Jesus forces a choice, a "crisis."
Will we be friends with Christ, or will we give our friendship to
the ruler of this world? Will we abide in Christ, or will we abide in
"the world"? This "crisis" reiterates the key theme of the Farewell
Discourse: going away is for the sake of love. We must cleave to
Christ and go with him out of "the world" in order to bear witness to him "that the world might be saved through him" (John
3:17). The Christian renounces "the world" for the sake of its
salvation. We judge the wickedness of the world, and we do so
out of love for the world.

In another recapitulation of his theme—going away is for the
sake of drawing near—Jesus reassures his disciples: "I tell you
the truth: it is to your advantage that I go away, for if I do not go
away, the Advocate will not come to you; but if I go, I will send
him to you" (John 16:7). The Farewell Discourse is shifting from
an anthropocentric to a theocentric perspective. Up to this point
Jesus has been teaching us about the spiritual union made possible
by his commandment of love. Through faith in him and in obedience to his commandments we can abide in him, which means
we can go with him to the Father, for whoever abides in the Son
abides in the Father. Put differently, in love and friendship with
Jesus we can go with him to the cross, even as he goes alone. In
fellowship with him we can bear witness to his love, even amid
the persecutions of this world. Now he speaks of the way in which
he will continue to abide in *us*, even as he goes away, rather than
we in him. The gone-away Jesus will send the Holy Spirit, who
will bind the disciples ever more closely to him. By the power of
the Holy Spirit, those who believe in Jesus will speak his words,

not their own. Their lives will glorify him. The Holy Spirit will "take what is mine and declare it to you" (16:15). The Advocate will clarify and give assurance to the faithful that they are indeed branches of the vine, beloved by the vinedresser.

The penultimate section of Jesus's address to his disciples recapitulates the central theme of distance for the sake of intimacy: "A little while, and you will no longer see me, and again a little while, and you will see me" (John 16:16). The disciples wonder what he is talking about. But the reader knows. Jesus is going down into the tomb. The world will rejoice, imagining that its regime of sin and death has triumphed. The disciples will sorrow, fearing that their beloved teacher has been taken from them forever. But the Lord's going away is for the sake of love's joyful return. The crucified Son of God will rise from the dead. "I will see you again," Jesus tells his disciples, who are confused by all this talk of going away that somehow involves drawing nearer still. "Your hearts will rejoice, and no one will take your joy from you" (16:22). As a woman rejoices in new life after the anguish of childbirth, the coming intimacy with the risen Son—and, in him, intimacy with the Father—will eclipse the dark distance of the cross.

"I have conquered the world!" Jesus concludes (John 16:33). This triumphant declaration on the way to the cross functions in the Gospel of John in the same way as does Jesus's statement at the end of the Gospel of Matthew, "I am with you always, to the end of the age" (Matt. 28:20). Both assert the same truth. As Paul says, "I am convinced that neither death, nor life, nor angels, nor rulers, nor things present, nor things to come, nor powers, nor height, nor depth, nor anything else in all creation, will be able to separate us from the love of God in Christ Jesus our Lord" (Rom. 8:38–39).

═══

No doubt this has been an altogether too superficial sketch of some of the most profound chapters of the New Testament. The

Gospel of John opens out in countless directions. The church fathers read these chapters as invitations to trinitarian reflection, and rightly so, while I've read them in a soteriological way, focusing on our participation in Christ, our at-one-ment with him, and through him with the Father. I've done so because it provides the most helpful background for an enriched ecumenical reading of John 17. Ecumenism has to do with the unity of the church— abiding with one another as friends in and of Christ. By my reading, John 17 is an important ecumenical text because it teaches us about the true nature of Christian unity—the "abiding" or at-one-ment that Christ's love seeks.

Now let's turn to John 17 and work our way patiently through the text. It is an extended prayer. This is important, because prayer seeks to abide in God. The very act of prayer presumes the presence of God. Prayer can be perfunctory and rote. But even when we address God with vague and half-hearted inner intentions, we are speaking as if he were near, as if he can hear us. For this reason, prayer always has the effect of "drawing near." This is true for even the most mechanical and routine prayers. And if by God's grace we are truly present in prayer, our hearts are open to communion with God. We converse with our Lord. We bring before him our concerns and share our lives with him. Prayer aspires to spiritual communion.

The same holds for the role of prayer in our common life together as Christians. When we pray for others, we join ourselves to them, making their concerns ours, sharing in their lives as we bring them before God. The corporate prayer of the church is thus an act of unity. At certain moments in the liturgy, the leader of the congregation prays on behalf of the entire community, making his voice the voice of the church. In the Catholic Church this union in prayer is most poignant during the sacrifice of the Mass. The priest speaks on behalf of the gathered faithful as he offers up the bread and wine. At the same time, he speaks on Christ's behalf as he repeats the words of institution. In the eucharistic prayer, therefore, the priest becomes the focal point of at-one-ment. He represents the congregation seeking God *and* God seeking his elect.

The prayer Jesus offers in John 17 has the same double function. He begins by petitioning the Father: "Glorify your Son so that the Son may glorify you" (17:1). Jesus is asking his Father to accept the sacrifice he desires to offer on our behalf. He wishes for the Father to call him to the cross, which is his glorification. On the cross the Son will demonstrate his "authority over all people" (17:2), and he will use that power, not for his own sake, but for the sake of those whom he loves. Jesus continues, "Father, glorify me in your own presence with the glory that I had in your presence before the world existed" (17:5). And what is the source of this eternal glory? It is the inner life of the Godhead, which John elsewhere teaches is love: "God is love" (1 John 4:8).

If we keep in mind the tensions between distance and unity that predominate in the Farewell Discourse, we can see how this passage of Scripture is pregnant with the trinitarian theology that would eventually be formulated by the church. Jesus is praying, in his human nature, that he and the Father should be one in will and purpose. He has been sent; the Father has sent him. Jesus has his own mission; he has accomplished the work the Father has given him (John 17:4). But they share in the same eternal glory (17:5). The Godhead is united through all eternity, and this union of divinity obtains even as there is a distinction of persons, even as the Son leaves the Father, a leaving that is for the sake of their unity in love.

As the prayer continues, Jesus shifts his focus, now speaking to the Father on behalf of his disciples whom he must now leave, a leaving also for the sake of his unity with them in love. In this shift—toward Christ as the bond of unity—we find a tacit theology of the church. It is my contention that the larger theme of union in love that suffuses the Farewell Discourse invites us to unpack this implicit ecclesiology. I propose to do so in the following terms.

Union in love is expressed (1) in apostolic continuity, (2) through the church as a countersign to the world's counterfeit modes of unity, (3) in sanctification, and (4) as a foretaste of the wedding banquet of the Lamb. I'll expound these four elements, not just dogmatically, but also as an exegetical meditation on the rest of John 17.

The Father has given the disciples into the care and love of the Son. Discharging this love is the "work" Jesus does, a work that has glorified both him and the Father. In prayer, Jesus specifies the nature of this work: "I have made your name known," and "the words that you gave to me I have given to them" (John 17:6, 8). This teaching has been effective: "They have kept your word" (17:6). The disciples have abided in Jesus's teaching, which is the Father's teaching, for the Son and the Father are one.

Before he goes to the cross, Jesus is present. He is there to keep his disciples true to the words he has taught them. He teaches with authority (Matt. 7:28–29). His authority guides his disciples, bringing them into conformity with his mind and mission. While he is with his disciples, Jesus personally oversees the continuity of his teaching. But he is leaving them to go to be glorified. And so Jesus petitions the Father: "Protect them in your name that you have given me, so that they may be one, as we are one" (John 17:11).

We can readily see the importance of this petition. Union in doctrine is vital for Christian unity. If we are at-one with the teachings Jesus has given us, then we will speak in one voice—his voice. Achieving doctrinal agreement here and now is thus rightly seen as a crucial goal of the ecumenical movement. It is also important to have unity through time. To say that our churches today teach in accord with the church of the apostles means that we are in unity with their teaching—Jesus's teaching. This continuity— unity through time—is what makes the church apostolic.

Unity in doctrine and faithfulness to the apostolic witness are key features of any sound theology of the church. By evoking these elements—unity here and now and unity across time—I don't think I am "imposing" doctrine in my interpretation of Jesus's petition. The plain sense seems clear. Jesus asks the Father to make the disciples at-one in their teaching. This requires them to abide in what he has given them, just as the Son abides in the Father, and the Father in the Son. Jesus is petitioning the Father to make his disciples of one mind and to oversee the apostolic faithfulness of the church's teaching through history. He is saying, "Just as I am eternally faithful to your truth—at-one with your word—keep my followers faithful."

It's important to see that the Father must *do something* in order to respond to Jesus's petition. And so he does. As we learn in the Acts of the Apostles, on the Feast of Pentecost the Father sends the Advocate, the Holy Spirit, who inspires the leaders of the church with a spirit of unity, a spirit of "abiding in." Guided by the Spirit, they teach with one voice, and they do so in accord with the word that has been given them. Later in Acts, we read about conflicts over divergent teachings concerning the early church's mission to the gentiles (Acts 15). To ensure unity, the Jerusalem Council comes to a common decision. The announcement of this decision is prefaced in a way that reflects the fact that the Father has answered Jesus's petition: "It has seemed good to the Holy Spirit and to us . . ." (15:28).

Christians in the West are divided about how to ensure that we are at-one with the revelation that Christ has given us. Catholics have a robust and precise doctrine of apostolic continuity. It specifies that bishops are successors to the apostles and that the bishop of Rome is the final arbiter of differences and disputes. The authority of the pope ensures unity. By contrast, Protestants rely on a Spirit-guided reading of Holy Scripture to secure unity in apostolic teaching, with confessional statements serving as tests or guides but not necessarily as final authorities. It's tempting for

a Catholic like me to point out that the Protestant approach hasn't
been very effective at maintaining unity. But I will refrain. Instead,
I want to focus on a typical Protestant objection to Catholic views
of the church's authority. This objection holds that the magisterial
apparatus—the church process by which doctrine is authoritatively defined—is not "in" Scripture. True, but consider Jesus's
petition: "Protect them in your name." Surely the Father, who loves
the Son and seeks to glorify him, will answer this petition. Thus,
whatever one thinks of the Catholic doctrine of papal primacy
and infallibility as defined by Vatican I, one must acknowledge the
integrity of its spiritual ambition. Catholic doctrine concerning
papal authority presumes that the Father has a superabundant love
for the Son. And the Father's love will do what it takes to ensure
continuity and unity—at-one-ment—in the Lord's name. Perhaps
the Father's love will even go so far as to guide the development
of a doctrine of apostolic authority beyond the bare specifics we
find in the New Testament.

"I have given them your word, and the world has hated them because they do not belong to the world, just as I do not belong to
the world" (John 17:14). Unity with and in Christ is a countersign
and offense to the world. This sharp opposition arises because the
world has its own principles of unity, its own empires and regimes,
and its own shared loves. These principles, regimes, and loves are
often not in themselves wrongful. The problem is that Rome and
her many successors present themselves as idols—authors and
guarantors of our happiness. Mammon reigns over many hearts
and organizes our lives. We are beckoned to abide in the marketplace or in the nation-state, in the Republic of Letters or in the
Halls of Science. Each has a proper, finite, and limited claim on
our souls. But all tend toward seduction, asking us to give them
our supreme loyalty, tempting us to consider them our highest
and final good.

Saint Augustine envisioned the company of the faithful as a city united in a common love of God. This unity guards against the seductions and temptations of the world. The church has apostles, prophets, teachers, workers of miracles, healers, helpers, administrators, and speakers in tongues (1 Cor. 12:28). They are among the many members of the one body of Christ, organized in a hierarchy so that they can be coordinated toward their common end, which is friendship with Christ. The church is a countersign, therefore, because she makes a transcendent claim on the loyalty of her members, ruling out submission to the principalities and powers that rule the world. The church has a creed to believe in, a constitution by which to govern her affairs, and a way of life that commands our loyalty. We do not abide in Christ in a merely spiritual or intellectual way. He has a body, a dwelling place with many rooms.

Catholic legalism, bureaucracy, and hierarchy are sometimes thought to be liabilities. But Jesus teaches that the church must be a countersign, and thus I think the opposite is true (at least most of the time). In the modern era, the Catholic Church has reorganized herself as an independent city distinct from the modern nation-state, the global marketplace, and our culture's medical-therapeutic complex. She has her own laws, her own diplomats, and even her own tiny plot of land in the middle of Rome. In this regard, the Catholic Church is the only significant, large-scale, and visible counter-regime in modernity, the only substantial form of life not organized by the economic, social, and political principles that reign in the West, and increasingly around the world.

———

Christian unity is not simply a goal to be achieved and an ideal to be championed, as if unity were merely the object of ecclesiastical diplomacy and bureaucratic planning. Jesus prays to the Father, "Sanctify them in the truth" (John 17:17). The truth to which he refers is that of unity: he and the Father are one. The logic of sanctification is woven into the notion of unity. To confess Jesus as the eternally begotten Son of God is to abide in him, acknowledging him as one with the Father. To abide in Jesus is to abide in the Father. Therefore, when petitioning God to sanctify us in the truth, Jesus is asking the Father to imprint upon us ever more deeply the truth of what we believe, to write it on our hearts. As he has taught throughout the Farewell Discourse, to believe in him is to go with him, and thus to go to the Father—to be at-one with the Father.

The goal is not Christian unity, at least not primarily. Jesus petitions the Father to sanctify us in the truth. That's the primary goal. The world does not come to believe because it sees divided Christians united. This is to confuse effect with cause. The world will believe because it sees us united with the living God, at-one with the Eternal. This does not mean Christian unity has no role to play. One cannot abide in Christ—and thus be sanctified in the truth—if one does not obey his commandment of love. And love seeks unity. Thus, to venture a restatement of Jesus's prayer, he petitions the Father to bring us to believe in him more deeply and, in believing in him, to seek unity in love, just as he and his Father enjoy an eternal unity in love.

If we think about unity and sanctification in this way, we can avoid a false chicken-and-egg dilemma. Must we pursue ecumenism in order to deepen our faith? Or do we need first to become more faithful so that we can do what needs to be done to achieve Christian unity? Neither way of thinking is fruitful, because they encourage what might be called ecumenical works righteousness. I note, moreover, that the false dilemma is largely unique to the divided Christian West. The rest of Christendom sees unity as something to be preserved or deepened rather than "achieved." One seeks unity within the already-existing unity of the church, however damaged by division; it is not something that is established or created.

There's something right about the circular logic of seeking unity within unity. For one needs unity to seek unity. We must be sanctified in the truth if we are to have any hope of practicing a genuinely Christian unity in the truth. But those who are sanctified in the truth abide in Christ's love, and thus they already participate in the unity that his love seeks. And so we must abide in an already-available unity—abide in Christ—in order to realize the not-yet-achieved unity we desire for our churches.

There are lessons to be drawn from the close relation between sanctification in the truth and entering into the unity of Christ's truth. One lesson concerns our ecumenical hopes. They are in vain if we do not first attend to the unity of our own communities. We need to practice unity locally, as it were, if we hope to achieve it globally.

The other lesson is descriptive. The modern ecumenical movement is not rooted in goodwill. And it certainly must not depend upon the quasi-Pelagian notion that we have an ecumenical duty to seek Christian unity. Instead, desire for unity flows from the ways in which Christians of different denominations have already tacitly and informally and haltingly found themselves to be at-one in Christ. This has happened in many ways. The late nineteenth-century missionary movement was a seminal instance of "found unity." In our time, shoulder-to-shoulder efforts in the pro-life movement and other cultural struggles have played an important role in drawing us together. As our post-Christian culture becomes more aggressive and arrogant, we will find an ever-greater unity as objects of the world's ire. There are other latent unities as well, more subtle but no less important. Modern theology, especially biblical studies, has been greatly influenced by the shared culture of modern academic life. This, too, can unite us. I'll venture that readers of this book are united in a late-modern dissatisfaction with modern methods of biblical exegesis, the dissatisfaction that motivated me to pen these reflections.

———

Jesus's final prayer for unity leans toward future consummation. He no longer prays for his disciples but instead addresses the

Father "on behalf of those who will believe in me through their word" (John 17:20). Jesus is referring to those who will come to faith because of the witness of those who believe in him. He continues by reiterating the promise of faith. To believe in him is to be united with him, and through him with the Father. Jesus asks "that they may all be one. As you, Father, are in me and I am in you, may they also be in us" (17:21). In this Christian at-one-ment with God in Christ, and in him with one another, the world will see God's truth. This truth—God is love—is what we see in the crucified Son who gives his life for his friends. It is the truth of the Father who sends him and raises him from the dead. All of this is made manifest in the shared faith of those who believe, "so that the world may believe that you have sent me" (17:21).

Jesus recapitulates and expands his hymn to the power of love. "The glory that you have given me I have given them" (John 17:22a). The glory referred to here is that of the cross and resurrection. It is the glory of election going back to Abraham, the glory of God's indomitable love that overcomes all obstacles, even sin and death. The Son has received this glory from all eternity. He now gives it to his disciples, and through them to all who believe in him. Earlier in the Farewell Discourse we've been told how this gift is given to us. The pearl of great price comes in the form of a new commandment: love one another as he has loved us.

Now comes the next step of the prayer. It is the passage so often quoted in ecumenical statements. The glory of love's desire for at-one-ment is given to those who believe "so that they may be one, as we are one" (John 17:22b). Jesus commands us to love so that we might become Godlike, firmly united with one another in love, just as he is united with the Father in love. He goes on to pray, in effect, "Let it be so, my Father": "I in them and you in me" (17:23a). This reiterates his desire to realize the at-one unity that God's love brings to the world. Jesus continues, stipulating that he desires love's union with his Father in order "that they may become completely one, so that the world may know that you have sent me and have loved them even as you have loved me" (17:23b). Jesus is praying that we might participate in the love that makes the Holy Trinity eternally at-one (17:24). Of course, in this life we never perfectly achieve at-one-ment. We are neither perfectly at-one with God in Christ nor at-one with one another in the gospel. However, insofar as we are at-one—united with God in Christ and with one another—we participate in the triune life of God. And in so doing, we abide in and enjoy a foretaste of love's triumph in the last days.

―――――

In my effort to read John 17, the guiding scriptural passage for modern ecumenism, I have glossed unity as at-one-ment. With this formulation I have suggested a connection between Christian unity and the doctrine of the atonement. I think this link is justified, not by philology or historical-critical speculation but by its exegetical fruitfulness. As I hope this exercise in theological exegesis has made clear, in the Gospel of John our union with God is intimately connected to our unity in Christ. The doctrine of the atonement is the theological tool by which we analyze how we are taken over the great chasm of sin to enter into fellowship with God. I once wrote a book on this topic, one that undertook no exegesis but instead operated in the realm of concepts and engaged the modern theological tradition.[2] In these exegetical reflections, I have not used the atonement theologies that are so richly developed in the West in my exegesis, at least not explicitly. But the logic of those theologies has operated in my mind as I have reflected on our Lord's words in John 17. How could it be otherwise? Our corporate union in Christ rests in our personal union with him. For this reason, the doctrine of the atonement sheds light on how God in his generosity will bridge the chasms that

2. R. R. Reno, *Redemptive Change: Atonement and the Christian Cure of the Soul* (Harrisburg, PA: Trinity Press International, 2002).

separate our churches. I am reinforced in this conviction by the fact that Saint Paul makes a connection between classical themes of atonement theology and unity in Christ (Eph. 2:11–22). I certainly have failed to say enough about this connection. But I hope I have planted the thought in the reader's mind that a doctrinally formed exegetical imagination can open up the Scriptures in fruitful ways.

7

LAW, LOYALTY, AND LOVE

THAT SENSITIVE SOULS LOOK upon social relations with dismay should not surprise us. When we link arms, we are capable of remarkable achievements. Family, city, and nation rightfully evoke powerful feelings of loyalty. But we know only too well that the misty eye of patriotism is often half-blind. The clear eye of social analysis sees that deep injustices often shadow our society. Every pyramid seems to have been built by slaves, not always lashed and driven by taskmasters whose dominion is outward and obvious but nevertheless in some way beholden to forces and powers that care little for the weal and woe of the multitudes who toil in anonymity. The glory of our collective achievements cannot silence the groans of affliction from those who labor in the hard service of brick and mortar.

It is a conceit of modernity that we are the first to hear the cry of the oppressed, the first to see the cruel realities of injustice. This is not true, of course. The prophets gave voice to God's judgment against those who "devour the poor" (Hab. 3:14). They denounced the restless greed of the mighty and reproved those who did not "aid the poor and needy" (Ezek. 16:49). The New Testament sustains these vigorous judgments against the haughty arrogance of the wealthy, who oppress the poor and drag them into court (James

131

2:6). Woe to those "dressed in purple and fine linen" (Luke 16:19), satiating themselves at banquets while ignoring the indigent who lie dying at their gates. The time of judgment has come. The Lord "has put down the mighty from their thrones," and "the rich he has sent empty away" (Luke 1:52–53 RSV). No, it cannot be said that our age is uniquely sensitive to poverty and oppression.

But, as moderns, we can justly claim novelty in at least one respect. We congratulate ourselves that we are *more* aware of injustice and, more important still, are uniquely poised to address it. We see injustices as structural, and therefore curable with well-planned reforms. We tell ourselves that social evils are the result of perverted social systems rather than the consequences of bad leaders and citizens with corrupt souls, a problem much more intractable than the defects of bad social design. We think about the suffering of the poor and the oppression of the weak almost exclusively against a background of social and economic conditions rather than in personal and spiritual terms. We fixate on the social construction of the "other," the hegemony of capital, the institutionalization of poverty, the culture of welfare dependency, the legacy of segregation, the perils of globalization and imperialism, and any number of other supposedly malevolent enterprises.

The conviction that morally serious responses to injustice and suffering must address so-called root causes unites these catchphrases and isms. In order to remove slavish conditions, we must reform the way we build pyramids! To that end, we establish social programs to ensure that there is enough straw to ease the making of bricks. Or, if we have a neoconservative bent, we advocate for enterprise zones for pyramid building and tax-rebate schemes for straw contractors. One way or another, our modern social conscience follows the now-current proverb: Feed a man a fish, and he'll eat for a day. Teach a man to fish, and he'll eat for a lifetime.

Well-designed social programs and targeted incentives have their value. I'm in favor of teaching men and women to fish rather than asking them to line up every morning for handouts. Yet I find myself wondering: Does our modern *social* conscience encourage a certain kind of moral blindness? As we focus on solving social problems by changing social structures, does the imperative of social change supersede moral formation as our highest priority? Are we tempted to imagine that we can reform society without curing our souls?

To guard against this temptation, I propose that we undertake a modest exercise in self-knowledge through an encounter with a differently formed conscience. William Langland is a mysterious late-medieval figure about whom we know very little, other than that he authored a remarkable poem, *Piers Plowman*. The poem is an artifact of a mind profoundly engaged with the social dysfunctions and injustices rampant in fourteenth-century England. Like the prophets, Langland was well aware of the rapine of the powerful and the sated indifference of the wealthy. And the poem is rich in social analysis that anticipates many aspects of our modern way of thinking. Yet Langland was not modern. *Piers Plowman* and its allegorical dream sequences offer a scriptural answer to the cry of the poor, not an answer grounded in social theory or economic analysis.

The source of Langland's outlook is found in Saint Paul's First Letter to the Corinthians. The occasion for this letter was a report (or reports) given to Paul of quarreling and dissensions in Corinth (1:10–11), communal spats spurred by jealousy and a spirit of strife (3:3). Identifying the precise nature of the conflict in Corinth has occupied biblical scholars, but the lay reader need not come to definite conclusions to see that Paul is concerned with problems of communal order and authority. The Corinthian community seems to have splintered into rival factions, and this disturbs him. Some say, "I belong to Paul"; others say, "I belong to Apollos"; still others claim, "I belong to Cephas" or "I belong to Christ" (1:12).

Living on the far side of doctrinal development in the church's early centuries, it is easy for the Christian reader to say that Paul is concerned about the unity of the church. This is not a false conclusion. But a too-hasty appeal to unity as a theological concept can cause us to miss the social argument that unfolds in 1 Corinthians. In chapters 5–12, Paul works through the dysfunctions afflicting the Corinthian community, identifying problems and proposing solutions. He addresses questions of sexual morality and purity, and he affirms the need for communal boundaries ("Drive out the wicked person from among you" [5:13]). He exhorts the Corinthians to "glorify God in your body" (6:20) by way of personal discipline (7:25–39) and clear communal standards (7:1–16). Rites of communal initiation and markers of membership are treated in a brief discussion of circumcision (7:18–19). In the longest section, Paul wrestles with the problem of idolatry, the mother of all communal disasters (8:1ff.). He then turns to scriptural laws concerning economic relations and the obligation to support religious teachers (9:1–10:33). This tour through the communal problems in Corinth concludes with a discussion of head coverings in worship, the proper disposition of the community during the celebration of the eucharistic meal, and the ordering of spiritual gifts (11:2–12:31, picking up again in 14:1–40).

A Jewish student of Talmud who reads the central chapters of 1 Corinthians may disagree with Paul's reasoning and conclusions. But he will find the idiom familiar. Paul plays fast and loose with crucial terms such as "temple" (see 3:16; 6:19; 9:13), and he appeals to Christ and the Eucharist (see 10:14–22), but his discourse remains within a recognizably Jewish tradition of legal reasoning. He addresses reports he has received about communal disputes and problems, and he conveys judgments that he wishes to be adopted by the Corinthians as authoritative. We might say, at least initially, that Paul's main solution to the problem of dissension, communal conflict, jealousy, and strife is to clarify and reinforce communal norms by relying on his own (to his mind, rightful) claim to authority as the one who interprets and applies the law.

Paul's reasoning aims at more than reestablishing order in Corinth. In his teaching, his commandments instruct and shape the community. They ensure the coordination and harmonization of different communal functions that are ordained by God and infused with providential purpose. In this regard, law does not just restrain evil; it guides the members of the church in Corinth toward the good. Paul insists that his authoritative decisions are "for your own benefit, not to put any restraint upon you, but to promote good order and unhindered devotion to the Lord" (1 Cor. 7:35). Law and order free the Corinthian Christians from a debilitating condition of conflict and dissension, not to ensure calm and cooperation for its own sake but so that each might run the race of self-control and receive the imperishable crown of sanctification that brings honor to the entire community (see 9:24–25).

To explain his sanctifying ambition, Paul appeals to the analogy of the body. "Just as the body is one and has many members, and all the members of the body, though many, are one body," he writes, "so it is with Christ. For in the one Spirit we were all baptized into one body—Jews or Greeks, slaves or free—and we were all made to drink of one Spirit" (1 Cor. 12:12–13). One might say that his dictates and judgments about communal norms express a "science of the body." The prescriptions are meant to restore the Corinthian body to health by ordering its members toward a common service of Christ, the head. In this ordering, questions of individual honor and status, inclusion and exclusion, must be subordinated to the larger communal project of drinking of the "one Spirit."

The analogy of the body provides more than an image of unity. It serves as a supple tool for social analysis. Paul uses the analogy to describe the atmosphere of grievance and enmity that characterizes the Corinthian church.

> If the foot would say, "Because I am not a hand, I do not belong to the body," that would not make it any less a part of the body. And

if the ear would say, "Because I am not an eye, I do not belong to the body," that would not make it any less a part of the body. If the whole body were an eye, where would the hearing be? If the whole body were hearing, where would the sense of smell be? But as it is, God arranged the members in the body, each one of them, as he chose. (1 Cor. 12:15–18)

As with the physical body, so it is with the church, a body politic. Each member is assigned a role. Some are called to be married, others to be unmarried (7:1–16). The mark of circumcision is assigned to some but not to others (7:18–19). Some serve as slaves, while others are free (7:21–24). In each instance, Paul urges the individual members to affirm their place in the larger body: "Let each of you lead the life that the Lord has assigned, to which God called you" (7:17; see also vv. 20, 24). The slave is no more to resent the master than the foot is to hold a grudge against the hand.

Paul is not writing a political treatise. Nevertheless, I think it's fair to say that the central chapters of 1 Corinthians and its culminating and extended analogy of the body in chapter 12 outline a social ethic of "stations and duties" governed by patriarchal authority—God's authority in theory, but Paul's law-giving communal authority in fact. "I am not writing this to make you ashamed," he says at the end of his extended opening justification of his boldness in writing to the Corinthians, "but to admonish you as my beloved children. For though you might have ten thousand guardians in Christ, you do not have many fathers. Indeed, in Christ Jesus I became your father through the gospel" (4:14–15). It was Paul who brought the Corinthians out of their affliction of spiritual confusion and into covenant with the Lord. The Corinthians should treat him as a new Moses, the authorized deputy of God who communicates a life-giving law.

With this account of authoritative law-giving to ensure a hierarchy of stations and duties, I have reached something of a rhetorical apex. I have conjured out of Paul's letter a patriarchal model of the social pyramid—one made permanent by appeal to divine providence ("Let each of you lead the life that the Lord has assigned") and capped by authority derived from God ("In Christ Jesus I became your father"). But having built up to this point, we must now fall down the other side. For Paul's social discourse takes a dramatic turn, and the turn suggests a disorienting dynamism that threatens to topple the sacred pyramid of patriarchal politics. He never denies the legitimacy of the pyramid; the hierarchical body of stations and duties is not revoked—and yet he subverts it. This combination, I submit, marks Christianity and its influence on the political cultures it encounters. The gospel affirms existing hierarchies *and* it softens them, even to the point of overturning them spiritually, if not politically.

As Paul develops his analogy of the body, he observes that God chastises the proud and raises up the lowly. Vital organs are vulnerable, and "the members of the body that seem to be weaker are indispensable" (1 Cor. 12:22). Things are not always as they seem, for outward appearances of importance and dignity can deceive. The itinerant, tent-making preacher who lacks the fine rhetorical skills of a public orator may be, against all the usual signs, the true communal authority—or so Paul suggests of himself in the opening chapters of 1 Corinthians. As a result, the Christian politics of the social body promotes a unique economy of honor. Paul observes, "Those members of the body that we think less honorable we clothe with greater honor, and our less respectable members are treated with greater respect; whereas our more respectable members do not need this" (12:23–24). Paul is giving social expression to the New Testament's great theme of reversal. As he puts it in his famous account of the kenosis of Christ, "He humbled himself and became obedient to the point of death—even death on a cross," and so on (Phil. 2:8; see also vv. 6–11). The

social implications of this reversal are made explicit in a number
of scriptural passages. For example:

> The LORD makes poor and makes rich;
>   he brings low, he also exalts.
> He raises up the poor from the dust;
>   he lifts the needy from the ash heap,
> to make them sit with princes
>   and inherit a seat of honor.
> For the pillars of the earth are the LORD's,
>   and on them he has set the world. (1 Sam. 2:7–8)

> He has shown strength with his arm;
>   he has scattered the proud in the thoughts of their hearts.
> He has brought down the powerful from their thrones,
>   and lifted up the lowly. (Luke 1:51–52)

These bold pronouncements of revolution bring us to the brink
of an inversion of the entire pyramid of hierarchy.

There can be no doubt that the gospel's kenotic pattern is socially explosive. It destabilizes the orderly world of stations and
duties overseen by patriarchal authority.[1] But Paul does not preach
revolution. He does not reorder social relations in Corinth (or
anywhere else, for that matter—see especially Rom. 13). Instead
of turning the body upside down and putting the feet on top, he
wants to make the machinery of hierarchy less cold and rigid. To
achieve this end, he pursues a rhetorical strategy that carefully
situates the kenotic pattern. "God has so arranged the body,"
he continues, "giving the greater honor to the inferior member"
(1 Cor. 12:24). This divine ordering is done not to raise the inferior
over the superior but, rather, so "that there may be no dissension
within the body, but the members may have the same care for one

---

1. The pattern of inversion is not just socially disruptive; it makes a mess of our
metaphysical intuitions as well. See Robert W. Jenson, *Systematic Theology*, vol. 1
(New York: Oxford University Press, 1997).

another" (12:25). A Christian "politics of the body" therefore inverts honor and status, not roles and functions. And it does so in order to establish a compensatory symbolic exchange. A kenotic distribution of honor softens and humanizes differences in power, wealth, and status rather than reordering them. The most obvious example concerns patriarchal marriage. Instead of overthrowing the subordination of women to men, Paul seems to be urging men to act like gentlemen—opening doors for and giving up seats to the weaker sex. At least that's my gloss on Ephesians 5:25.

Perhaps Paul is aware that this purely symbolic domestication of the kenotic pattern is unsatisfactory. In any event, he breaks off his extended use of the analogy of the body very abruptly, urging the Corinthians to seek "greater gifts" and promising to teach "a still more excellent way" (1 Cor. 12:31). What follows this promise is one of the most famous and oft-quoted portions of the New Testament: the hymn to love (chapter 13).

We do not need to fathom the mysteries of the Pauline theme of love in order to see the role that this move plays in his social vision. The turn to the more excellent way of love internalizes the kenotic pattern and locates its revolutionary consequences within the soul. Love does not overturn the law and its hierarchies of duties and responsibilities, nor does it smash the social pyramid that places some above and others below. Much to the dismay of modern social reformers, the kenotic revolution takes place within rather than without. Love lubricates power relations with the spiritual desire to serve rather than the carnal desire to be served. Infused with love, the members of the social body do not renounce their stations and duties; they seek to outdo one another in selflessness.

With this formulation, some might accuse me of reading Paul through the lens of the medieval synthesis that Langland reiterates again and again in *Piers Plowman*: law, loyalty, and love working in harmony. *Law* defines and regulates the three estates—priests, knights, and laborers—ensuring that they work in harmony according to their divinely appointed roles. The priestly caste conveys the holy mysteries, teaches according to revealed truth, and through the power of pardon secures right relation to God. Knights punish the wicked, protect the social body, and enforce the law. The laboring estate secures the necessities for physical survival by tilling the land. *Loyalty* keeps each in his place. Members of the three estates are pledged to their stations and duties: priests and knights by explicit oath, and laborers by humble acceptance of their roles. Finally, *love* animates all, securing constant renewal of the social system through kenotic acts of charity that compensate for the inevitable failures of law and loyalty.

I plead guilty to the charge. The interesting question, however, is whether I am "imposing" this medieval scheme onto Paul's letter. Perhaps the medieval notions grew out of a perceptive reading of Paul. And perhaps that reading has a great deal to teach us about social reform and renewal.[2] I'll argue that it did and does. To make my case, we need to turn to Langland and *Piers Plowman*.

At first glance, William Langland's *Piers Plowman* seems nothing like Paul's First Letter to the Corinthians. The poem is a sequence of allegorical dreams that are like real dreams in their sudden, unexpected shifts in focus, their many loose ends, the appearance and disappearance of characters without advance notice, and their long, confusing digressions. Yet the dreams also manifest vivid social realism.

For a reader with prejudgments about the nature and function of allegory, this realism is surprising. The complaint against allegory is that it is "ahistorical" and does little more than dress up abstract ideas in the clothing of character and the semblance of action. Perhaps this is true for some allegories, but in *Piers Plowman* the dreams have lively dialogue and realistic social interactions, so

2. For an elaboration of the medieval social and political ideal amply illustrated with citations from medieval sermons and religious literature, see G. R. Owst, *Literature and Pulpit in Medieval England* (New York: Barnes and Noble, 1966), esp. 548–75.

much so that interpreters have difficulty pinning down the meaning of the allegorical figures, which suggests that Langland's allegories are not entirely allegorical. The title character, Piers the Plowman, appears to represent the earnest Christian at the outset of the poem. But by the end he seems to represent Christ and the church. What remains constant, however, is the social reality depicted. When Piers sets about to cultivate his half acre, the ale-drinking workers, shameless beggars, and public-house gossip are vividly portrayed. It is not always clear what one is supposed to think about the dreams. But most of the time it is easy to picture the social situations and interpersonal dynamics.

These situations and dynamics follow the Pauline pattern closely. Langland treats society as a body composed of different members established by God in a coordinated hierarchy. Like Paul, he faces a social body diseased by disorder. Unlike Paul, he does not claim communal authority. Nevertheless, he suggests a solution to social dysfunction. And that solution, again following Paul, involves the diffusion of the disposition of love, especially among the authorities responsible for maintaining social order. Langland organizes imaginative social discourse in *Piers Plowman* in the same way that Paul structures his social discourse in 1 Corinthians, communicating the same vision of communal harmony and flourishing. Or so I will argue.

The poem is divided roughly in half. The first portion mainly offers a diagnosis of the problems of social disorder. Scholars call this part the *visio*, because the narrator is largely a passive observer. The second section suggests the path to social renewal. This part is called the *vita*, because the narrator is an active participant in a quest for righteous living. The dreams that make up the poem are complex, and Langland's method of social analysis is circular. Or perhaps it is better to say that his analysis spirals toward its conclusion as he returns again and again to his main themes: the corruption of the clergy, the lassitude and base impulses of the peasantry, and the distracted impotence of the nobility. I will do my best to respect the unsystematic nature of the poem as I draw out its Pauline social teaching.

Langland begins with an evocation of the body politic structured by established stations and prescribed duties. Will, the narrator and dreamer, "went forth into the world wonders to hear," and "on a May morning on Malvern Hill" he falls asleep (prol.4).[3] In his dream he sees the Tower of Truth on the hilltop and the deep Dale of Death. Between them he beholds "a fair field full of folk" (prol.15–20). The field is this world. Viewing the crowd at a distance, the dreamer identifies the three estates of society: "some put themselves to the plough," others wear the bright clothes of nobility, and still others occupy themselves "in prayers and penances" (prol.22–32). All is as a medieval reader might picture a harmonious, well-functioning society.

Langland never deviates from the medieval notion of three estates. Later in the poem, he reiterates the threefold division of society (9.1ff.). The hardy peasant is to stay home. Knights and kings are to defend holy church and to rule righteously. Priests and bishops should chastise the wicked and to the penitent pardon provide. These are medieval platitudes that Langland neither mocks nor criticizes. Yet, in the prologue, the dreamer sees something that does not fit into the standard medieval theory of a threefold social body. There are folk not integrated into the system. They are not hapless helots but powerful social actors: "some chose trade—they thrive the better" (prol.33).

It is telling that the mention of trade (and its advantages) marks a shift in perspective in the first and stage-setting dream of the

3. There are three versions of *Piers Plowman*, which scholars label A, B, and C. The C-text is the final and longest version. The quotations provided are my modernizations of Langland's archaic English as found in the edition of the C-text prepared by Derek Pearsall, *Piers Plowman by William Langland* (Berkeley: University of California Press, 1978), and I provide citations in parentheses by passus and line.

poem. The dreamer is suddenly thrust into the hurly-burly of the field of folk, and what looks like a well-functioning social body at a distance is a mess when viewed up close. Minstrels invent salacious stories. Beggars fill their bags, their fat bellies belying their claims of poverty. Pilgrims and palmers turn their journeys into great getaway parties. Pardoners pursue profit, and parish priests sing for simony and sweet silver. The same holds for the workings of the king's court. Lawyers at the bar chase pennies and pounds, not justice. Instead of a society harmoniously ordered toward the common good, the dreamer sees communal decline greased by the ready availability of tempting money.

The prologue ends with a marvelous recapitulation of the opening depiction of the dreamer's journey from abstract and remote ideals of harmony to concrete and immediate experiences of disorder and dysfunction. At a distance, the dreamer sees the great diversity of folk: barons, burgers, and bondsmen; bakers, brewers, and butchers; tailors, tanners, and tillers of soil. In my mind's eye, I see a Norman Rockwell painting. But up close the people are touting their wares, tempting one another toward gluttony and excess in order to stimulate trade (prol.220–31). Suddenly, Rockwell's gauzy main street resolves into a hard-edged tract against consumerism, a National Public Radio segment casting aspersions on McMansions and anguishing over the American culture of conspicuous consumption.

There's something to the contemporary analogy. It is correct to read *Piers Plowman* as a brief against social trends taking hold in Langland's day. He lived in the second half of the fourteenth century, a time of important changes in medieval life. The two pillars of medieval society, the nobles and the clergy, were tottering. England was embroiled in an ongoing (and eventually failed) campaign to become the dominant force in France. The expenses of warfare drained the treasuries of the great lords. Knights were willing to sell their services, and local nobility were greedy for revenue. Captive to dynastic politics, the papacy had been moved

to Avignon, and in the late fourteenth century a restored papacy
in Rome competed with Avignon for legitimacy. The great men-
dicant movements of the twelfth century had run their course.
Langland often laments the corrupt state of the clergy and the
large number of irregular friars on the roads and in towns who beg
in order to avoid work. Nobility disarrayed and clergy corrupted,
the common people are without leadership. Without guardians,
good examples, and conscientious confessors, they descend into
disordered vices.

Langland does not simply describe all this. He also diagnoses,
and he analyzes the causes of social decay in ways that conform to
the modern scholarly consensus about the effects of social change
in late-medieval society. The emerging mercantile economy of the
growing cities and market towns undermined the earlier economy
of manor houses and yeoman agriculture. Langland dramatizes
the disruptive effects of the new wealth of commerce in the allegory of Meed the Maiden ("meed" is an old English word that
denotes reward, wage, or recompense for labor, but it can also
mean a bribe). She wreaks havoc with her alluring beauty.[4] Clergy
fall victim to simony. Knights and noblemen neglect their duties and chase after her. Merchants regret their losses more than
their sins. Justice is bought and sold. Usury, avarice, theft, lying,
envy, and richly decorated pride flourish. Everyone ogles Meed
the Maiden, lusting after her with corrupting desire.

In the allegory, Meed the Maiden is captured and brought before the king. As a righteous but worldly-wise ruler, the king would
like to harness this lovely lady to the task of just governance.
Angling to bring Meed the Maiden under the sway of justice, he
urges Conscience to marry her. But Conscience knows the ways of
such a woman. She is fickle and has ruined many men, and thus
Conscience refuses. He will not be mismatched. What, then, is

4. The story of Meed the Maiden is the longest, most tightly organized and unified
portion of *Piers Plowman*. It extends from passus 2 through passus 4.

the king to do? Here, Langland seems to anticipate a reactionary solution. Should the king not banish Meed the Maiden from his kingdom? This would allow him to root out the profit motive and stymie the emerging commercial economy, restoring honor and loyalty as the glue that holds society together.

After giving voice to the conceit that the king can restore the old ways, Langland allows Meed the Maiden to speak in her own defense. She offers what in present terms might be called neoconservative observations about society.

> It becomes for a king that shall keep a realm
> To give men meed that meekly him serves,
> To aliens and to all men, to honor him with gifts;
> Meed makes him be beloved and held as a man.
> Emperors and earls and all manner of lords
> Through gifts have servants to run and ride.
> The pope and all prelates presents accept
> And give meed to men to maintain their laws.
> Servants for their service meed they ask
> And take meed of their masters as by agreed accord.
> Both beggars and beadsmen crave meed for their prayers;
> Minstrels for their minstrelsy ask for their meed;
> Masters that teach clerks crave their meed;
> Priests that preach and the people teach
> Ask for meed and mass-pennies and their meals as well.
> All craftsmen crave meed for their apprentices;
> Merchandise and meed must go together.
> There is no lad that lives that loves not meed
> And glad to grasp her, great lord or poor. (3.264–82)

Needless to say, the king, the allegorical voice of social authority, is taken aback. "By Christ," he says, "Meed is worthy, me thinks, her mastery to have" (3.283–84). Langland is a social realist. Those whose duty is to govern are not at liberty to live in the pristine world of our ideals. As fungible wealth becomes a powerful social force, we cannot wish it away. Somehow, Meed the Maiden's ability to motivate must be brought into the service of the common good.

What, then, is the solution? How can social harmony be restored in a world in which sweet silver so readily seduces? The elaborate allegorical dream concludes with Langland's subtle suggestions about what will not work. Conscience goes to fetch Reason, who puts Wrong on trial, while Meed winks at the lawyers and sows corruption and confusion. The machinery of justice breaks down. The king is exasperated. He dismisses the legal system, which can be bought and sold. Perhaps Langland wishes his readers to see that a restoration of social harmony cannot be attained through carefully designed institutions, a warning to those of us who imagine we can cure injustices through "systemic change." Juries can be manipulated and judges bought, just as congressmen can be lobbied and districts gerrymandered. When wisdom and integrity are in short supply, institutional actors falter and the system breaks down. And so, the allegory ends with the king installing Reason as his chief chancellor and Conscience as the arbiter of justice in all the courts. The only way to justice, it seems, is to ensure that the magistrate has a well-ordered soul. We need something akin to Plato's philosopher king.

———

I have already noted the spiraling movement of the poem. A later allegorical episode echoes and extends the story of Meed the Maiden. Piers the Plowman has organized a commune on his half acre. Diggers do their digging, and workers do their working. Piers pays them a fair wage, and the farm flourishes. In an amusing image of Rousseau's ideal of the rustic life, a knight arrives, asking to be taught how to plow. But wise Piers turns him away. He must stay loyal to his place in the social body: "Keep holy church and myself from wasters and from wicked men who this world spoil" (8.26–27). All are to remain in that state of life to which God has called them, and insofar as they do, Piers's half acre remains the orderly social body envisioned by Paul, a well-functioning hierarchy (see 8.111–20). But the harmony soon breaks down. During lunch the workers drink too much ale. Shysters pretend to be lame (or deliberately maim themselves!) in order to gain alms and avoid work. Petty thieves raid the barn, and the knight proves incompetent. It seems that law and loyalty alone—each doing the proper task for the station to which he is called—cannot hold society together.

In the allegory, Piers the Plowman calls in an outside force, Sir Hunger, the negative image of Meed the Maiden. Sir Hunger squeezes the bellies of the wasters and batters the lazy workers with the pain of want. The positive effects are immediate. Not only are the workers motivated to return to work, but Sir Hunger also sobers the drunkards and drives the sham beggars back to honest employment. The pain of want seems to give Sir Hunger a Jesus-like power: "Blind and broke-legged he bettered by the thousand" (8.188)! But unlike Jesus, Sir Hunger provides no lasting cure. He is so effective in motivating self-reform on the half acre that a good harvest is forthcoming, and amid abundance the commune falls apart yet again, for all use their gains as an occasion to return to vice. Like the carrot of Meed the Maiden, the stick of Sir Hunger is morally impotent. Society cannot run on self-interest. Neither hope of reward nor fear of punishment can bring the social harmony Langland thinks necessary for human flourishing. Vice can be overcome only by virtue.

Not any virtue will do, however. Although Langland may echo Plato in treating the health of society as dependent upon the virtue of the magistrate (or, in the case of the half acre, the virtue of the laborers), he does not adopt a classical model of the well-ordered soul. For Langland, as for Paul, in order to function harmoniously the social body must be leavened by the kenotic pattern of selfless service. Sin draws society toward the disorder and dysfunction born of self-love; self-sacrifice moves collective life toward harmony and health. And, as did Paul, Langland interprets the Bible's many reversals of high and low, rich and poor, as symbolic exchanges of honor, not as mandates for social revolution.

The central reversal comes when Langland depicts suffering as a spiritual honor. This is a commonplace in any culture shaped by Christianity. Those who suffer most from ill fortune and injustice are the closest to God, as the Sermon on the Mount makes clear: Blessed are the poor, for theirs is the kingdom of heaven. Suffering remains a social evil that requires prudent action by those in power. As we've seen, Langland wishes for wise leaders who will promote the common good. But suffering is also a spiritual gift that should be honored by society. The meek shall inherit the earth, and this means that the powerful do well to pay homage to those who are emblems of God's foreordained heirs. In this regard, the corporeal works of mercy are supplemented—perhaps superseded—by symbolic exchanges of status. Those on top paradoxically look up to those on the bottom: the poor, the hungry, and the oppressed. As Paul suggests with the analogy of the body, this kenotic inversion of the usual patterns of honor renews the hierarchical system by promoting reciprocity and mutual dependence.

Langland's digression into the role of the mentally ill provides insight into his understanding of kenotic inversion and its role in restoring social harmony. Those who lack wit, lunatic lollers who leap about and go mad at the moon, are holy fools (see 9.105–10). They are secret disciples who, in their debility, fulfill Christ's command: "Greet no one on the road" (Luke 10:4). By their lack of mental coherence, they follow Paul's advice: "If you think that you are wise in this age, you should become fools so that you may become wise" (1 Cor. 3:18). But most of all, the disabilities of the wandering mentally ill and other social misfits signify the perfect poverty of body and spirit that is a mark of apostolic integrity (9.19–120).

As icons of Christlike purity, those suffering from mental ailments provide an exemplary opportunity for a kenotic politics of symbolic exchange. In Langland's view, the wealthy have a duty to use their abundance to repair hospitals, bridges, and roads and to support schools, almshouses, and monasteries (9.30–36). The powerful must exercise civic responsibility, remembering that from those who have been given much, much is expected. But this does not require kenosis. It is the ethic of *noblesse oblige*. The wealthy can discharge these material duties at a distance, preserving their haughty sense of honor and maintaining their inaccessibility at the top of the social pyramid. However, when the high and mighty encounter the most impoverished members of society, the distance of honor and dignity must be renounced. The rich are to offer hospitality to the lowly street people of Langland's day: "Welcome and worship and with your goods help" (9.135). Here, the point is not that the fortunate have a duty to set the needy on the path toward upward mobility—to teach them to fish. The abject are to be integrated into society through social practices of gift giving and hospitality. They are to be honored in their poverty, not cured of it.

Langland often follows his exhortations to honor the poor with long diatribes against fake friars and others who put on the sad face of hunger in order to exploit charity and avoid work. These polemics indicate how important the Pauline kenotic reversal of honor is for his social vision. Just as false coins corrupt trade and undermine currency, the undeserving poor corrupt the kenotic pattern by debasing the spiritual honor of true poverty.

In this regard, Langland was typical. The medieval world was extraordinarily preoccupied with poverty—more so, I think, than is our own age of economic reform and revolution. Those in Langland's era and before gave detailed accounts of the nature of poverty: its spiritual significance and its degrees. They established criteria by which spiritual poverty can be distinguished from a false, worldly, and carnal poverty. It is telling, for example, that the thirteenth century was inflamed over the question of whether Christ had a purse. The symbolic economy of poverty, especially

its ability to signify saving truths, was a pressing medieval concern, not the material economy of poverty (root causes, social
conditions, and so forth) that preoccupies us. Modern readers find
Piers Plowman appealing because the poem seems to manifest a
"social conscience" and concern about the "little guy." However,
in Langland's telling, poverty and suffering are not problems to
be solved. The poor are "to take [their] misfortunes meekly and
mildly at heart" (9.183). As Jesus reminds his followers, "You always have the poor with you" (Matt. 26:11). Instead of mounting
a "war on poverty," Langland faithfully represents the medieval
consensus. Poverty is a curse, yes; there's no softening the pain of
want. But it is also a beatitude that contributes spiritual gifts to
society. Those who suffer need the corporeal works of mercy. But
they also need to be integrated into society so that their beatitude
can bring benefits to the entire body politic.

───────

The kenotic pattern of honoring those who suffer takes on its full
restorative, socially redemptive power insofar as it is internalized
and becomes an imperative of the soul. The second half of *Piers
Plowman*, the so-called *vita*, depicts a complex quest for ascend-
ing degrees of moral and spiritual formation: Do-Well, Do-Better,
and Do-Best. This part of the poem is complex, and scholars offer
different schemes for organizing the material. But the final destination of the quest is clear. Langland follows Paul and champions
love as the more excellent way. "Love and loyal belief hold life and
soul together" (17.22). The same holds true for society.

Langland's extended use of the parable of the Good Samaritan
illuminates. He uses this story from the Gospels to exposit 1 Corinthians 13, the hymn to love's excellence. Charity is the great
and renewing social virtue that supersedes justice and prudence.
The executive virtue of the well-ordered soul, charity plays the
same role in a well-ordered society (19.46–94). There is a law of
entropy in our fallen world. The friction of social interaction and

inevitable failures of justice are always draining moral energy out of the social body. The law that coordinates the three estates decays. As Langland sees so clearly, in his own time the new mercantile economy places great pressure on the social order, accelerating the ill effects of greed. There are ever highwaymen waiting in the hedges (or in the chancery; Langland never tires of criticizing the debilitating social consequences of corrupt clergy). Society is always in need of a Good Samaritan, a person whose actions are not defined by his or her social role but instead spring from love's selfless service. Just as Christ brings new life to a dying world through his self-emptying on the cross, so also does the kenotic love of his followers refresh the social order and bring peace.

Langland was not writing biblical commentary in verse. And he certainly did not devise his politics of love in order to outline something so dauntingly modern as a treatise on the political theology of the apostle Paul. But there can be no doubt that he was imbued with the Pauline view of society as a body of hierarchically ordered members perpetually renewed by their unity in love. *Piers Plowman* is Scripture-shaped, a poem written by a man whose imagination was formed by a Christian culture rooted in biblical interpretation.

Here we come to another deep ditch that we must cross. The Bible's political vision of hierarchy made mobile and humane by love's lubrications has become largely inaccessible to us. Our modern outlook is formed by "life, liberty, and the pursuit of happiness," not "law, loyalty, and love." We cannot reason scripturally about politics—at least not with Paul and Langland as our guides—because our moral imaginations recoil from the corporatism and hierarchy implied in the analogy of the body, an analogy that plays a central and indispensable role in the Bible's account of communal life. We are suspicious (if not contemptuous) of patriarchal authority, no matter how deeply infused by kenotic love it may be. And we distrust promises of spiritual renewal, thinking them excuses for inaction, if not screens behind which the powerful hide their real interest in maintaining position and privilege. We seek social change, not changes of heart.

I do not exempt myself. To be modern is to be foredoomed to many myopias, of which our crimped political imagination is but one. But we are not without hope of illuminations. At the end of the *visio* portion of *Piers Plowman*, the dreamer-narrator awakens. He finds himself "meatless and moneyless in the Malvern Hills" (9.297). Like the dreamer in Langland's poem, we often find ourselves meatless and moneyless in our late-modern Malvern Hills. But in this poverty of not knowing what to say and think about the injustices we face in the twenty-first century, we can find a blessing. Emptied of our vain conceits about being "change agents," perhaps we can hear anew Jesus's words in the Sermon on the Mount.

AN EXEGETICAL POSTMORTEM

IT WAS PROBABLY THE LATE 1990s, although I can't remember for sure. I was eating breakfast, sitting across the table from Rodney Clapp. We were in Charleston, South Carolina, for a conference sponsored by the Society for the Engagement of Anglican Doctrine. Rodney had recently been hired to launch the Brazos imprint for Baker. We were talking about publication ideas. I said impulsively, "What we really need is a commentary series written by theologians rather than biblical scholars." Rodney jumped out of his seat. "Yes, let's do it!" But I shook my head and demurred. It seemed a fantastical idea.

Yet the idea would not go away. In those days, Ephraim Radner, George Sumner, Chris Seitz, and I constituted something of a latter-day rat pack of recusants in the Episcopal Church. We were part of a wider circle of (at that point) younger theologians that included Bruce Marshall, Mike Root, David Yeago, Joe Mangina, Kendall Soulen, and others who were trying to sustain the authority of Scripture and the creeds in mainline Protestantism.

All of us had done our graduate studies at Yale University during the heyday of the so-called Yale School. Our teachers were proposing a "postliberal theology." Something like the Brazos Theological Commentary on the Bible series was perhaps an inevitable outgrowth of this milieu. Not coincidentally, four of the six editors of the Brazos series had studied at Yale in the 1980s, while the two more senior scholars, Robert Jenson and Robert Wilken, were closely associated with postliberal theology. I recently reviewed a prospectus for the Brazos series and a version of the guidelines provided to authors. In those documents, the term "intratextual" appeared quite often. That buzzword is a sure sign of Yale School influence. In order to gain a better sense of the achievements and limitations of the Brazos series, it's worth considering elements of this postliberal background.

═══════

In 1973 Hans Frei published *The Eclipse of Biblical Narrative*. In that book, he tells the story of the modern transition from "precritical" to "critical" readings of Scripture. By his account, the deepest implication of the change concerns the subject matter of interpretation. For the precritical reader, the "literality" of the Bible—what is said in the text—serves as the stable focal point. Augustine, Aquinas, Luther, and others may have disagreed about how to read various passages, but they agreed that good exegesis means expounding what is said in Matthew 5, for example, or in the prologue to the Gospel of John.

By contrast, modern readers treat the Bible as a body of evidence, and their goal is to use that evidence to reason their way to something deemed more fundamental than what the text says. For historical critics, the "something more" might be the events that actually occurred. Writing about the historical Jesus is a clear instance of this approach. Or critical scholars use material from Exodus in order to hypothesize about the nature of ancient Israelite religion. Or they read Paul's letters in order to gain insight into the beliefs and practices of first-century Christian communities. As I noted in chapter 4, the pressures generated by doctrinal controversies were already driving the Reformation-era theologians to speculate about the historical context of the letters of Paul and

James. But in the main, Frei is correct. Premodern readers of the Bible read so as to get "inside" the text rather than trying to see what is "behind" it.

Modern theologians have a different agenda than do historical critics, but they, too, often read the Bible to get to something else. Influenced by Schleiermacher, modern liberal theologians seek to discern in Scripture a pattern of religious feelings. Yes, the Gospels tell us about the life and work of Jesus. But they do so in order to generate in us a response, and it is the response that is revelatory, not the text. Or the liberal theologian distills from the text a moral pattern purportedly exemplified in Jesus's life and teaching. Modern readers who have a theologically conservative cast of mind often search the Scriptures for evidence in favor of ancient creeds and traditional doctrines. Or they contend with modern critics over the historical accuracy of the biblical narrative. What the Bible says becomes a means for proving or supporting something else, whether conceived of in "liberal" or "conservative" terms.

The Eclipse of Biblical Narrative is an ambiguous work. Frei writes as an intellectual historian, not a theologian, although the theological implications are subtly underlined throughout. The book gave rise to something called "narrative theology," which was also an ambiguous phenomenon. But seeds were planted. In demonstrating his main thesis, Frei shows that modern exegesis atomizes the Bible into a body of evidence for something else. For example, the historical critic sifts through the Gospel of John to develop an account of the Johannine community, while the critic who is more theologically motivated wishes to demonstrate the "high Christology" supposedly found in this Gospel. As a consequence, argues Frei, the modern church loses touch with the "history-like narratives" of the Bible, the narrative flow of events that carries the reader through chapter after chapter, even book after book.

One could say that Frei wanted to recover the Bible in its "long" or narrative (there's that word again) form. This desire resonated with the work of another eminent Yale professor of that era, Brevard Childs. Although Childs did not use the term "canonical criticism," he argued for an approach that keeps the canon as a whole in mind as we read and interpret discrete portions of Scripture. He wanted to recover a classical exegetical imperative: Use Scripture to interpret Scripture!

The heyday of narrative theology was in the 1970s. It fizzled out fairly soon thereafter. The formal aspect of Frei's work that emphasized intensive reading, which is to say interpretation that seeks to get "inside" Scripture, had a more lasting influence. If I may be permitted Saint Augustine's distinction between use and enjoyment, on Frei's account modern readers "use" the Bible to get to what they think really matters—the actual historical events, the original community of composition and reception, the religious myth or feelings, or theological doctrines. By contrast, premodern readers "enjoy" the Bible. They read in order to relish the depths of God's Word. One can say, therefore, that postliberal theology sought to recover enjoyment, which means allowing Scripture to illuminate the enigmas of history, dogma, and religious experience rather than the other way around. As George Lindbeck put it, the biblical text "absorbs the world, rather than the world the text."

That famous line comes from *The Nature of Doctrine*, a small volume that defies easy categorization.[1] But I'd like to draw out an implication of Lindbeck's argument. The biblical text has been absorbing the world ever since it has been read as the Word of God. As a consequence—I've reiterated this point a number of times in this book—the church's language and practice are not so much derived from Scripture as shaped by and ordered toward it. Because this is so, the mind of a person whose thoughts are formed by the church's doctrine and whose sensibilities are governed by the church's liturgies will be attuned to Scripture's most powerful

1. George A. Lindbeck, *The Nature of Doctrine: Religion and Theology in a Postliberal Age* (Philadelphia: Westminster, 1984). The famous line is on page 118.

and consequential meanings. Put more simply: the church schools us to read Scripture well. This is so because (if you will indulge my use of an Aristotelian concept) Scripture is the church's formal cause.[2]

I have been too brief (and no doubt too obscure) in this account of postliberalism in theology. In this respect I am not atypical. Those who studied under Hans Frei and George Lindbeck have a reputation for making formal statements and avoiding the usual theological words and phrases that help us categorize a theologian's position. The very word "postliberalism" is formal— theology after liberal Protestantism. I need to say more, then, about this important influence on the Brazos series. In the interests of shedding a clearer light, let me draw out the postliberal influence as sharply as I can by anticipating objections to the Brazos series.

———

Crypto-fundamentalism is the most likely objection. The first volume to appear in the series was the Acts of the Apostles, commented upon by Jaroslav Pelikan. He was a vigorous correspondent, and he often sent me notes updating me on his progress. On one occasion, Pelikan recounted a comment made by the exasperated French prime minister Georges Clemenceau during World War I: "War is too important to leave to the generals." Pelikan went on to observe that the same applies to exegesis and historical critics. I deployed this witticism in my general introduction to the series, using it as a punchy way to justify turning to theologians for exegesis rather than to biblical scholars.

The jab was not well received by my brethren laboring in the vineyards of Old and New Testament studies. They see themselves as custodians of scriptural literacy and exegetical objectivity.

2. The notion of Scripture as the church's formal cause is implicit in Lindbeck's persistent use of the metaphor of grammar in *The Nature of Doctrine*.

They guard against literalism and anachronism—in their eyes the grave fundamentalist threats. The problem is this, however. Sharp rhetoric aside, the basic thrust of Pelikan's observation is unavoidable. It follows directly from Hans Frei's central thesis, which was that, however pious and deeply immersed in the canon the modern scholar may be, modern biblical studies is not concerned with the biblical text in itself but rather aims to gain a view of something else *by way of* the biblical text. Historical-criticism wants to understand the social contexts of composition, the history of reception, the textual sources, and editorial processes. The Bible serves as the means to those ends. Thus, like generals, modern biblical scholars undoubtedly make important contributions. But they're not to be trusted as high priests of exegetical integrity. In truth, modern traditions of reading may have created more problems than they have solved. One of those problems is fundamentalism. It is a proof-texting approach to the Bible that shares with the modern historical-critical methods a common empiricist approach that seeks "evidence."

This leads me to say that the Brazos series is the very opposite of fundamentalist. The series does not reject modern biblical scholarship. A number of commentators in the series make effective use of recent insights. In my own reading of Genesis, I appeal to the redaction criticism that illuminates the Priestly tradition behind the opening verses, a scholarly insight that reinforces rather than undermines the traditional translation, "In the beginning." No, what the Brazos series rejects is the modern scholar's claim to final authority over interpretation. I'll be the first to admit that this rejection makes the project "anti-modern." But that's fine with me, since fundamentalism is a modern phenomenon, and I'm happy to put that behind us.

Imposition of theological schemes is another objection. The Brazos series not only rejects the final authority of modern biblical

scholarship; it also disputes a rigid distinction between exegesis
and theology. In his 1974 commentary on Exodus, Brevard Childs
followed the approach that a Bible commentary series sponsored by
Eerdmans subsequently called "two horizons."[3] A commentary is
not complete, this approach argues, without theological reflection
on the determinations made by the modern exegete. The Brazos
series takes a quite different tack. Its aim is to undertake exegesis
informed by theology rather than basing theology on exegesis.

In this respect, the Brazos series is "anti-Protestant." The assumption that exegesis comes before theology gains credibility from a Protestant anxiety about the trustworthiness of the
church's teaching. This assumption was reinforced by modern
empiricism and its claim that we must provide data-anchored
foundations for knowledge. By my reading, the postliberalism
pioneered by Frei and Lindbeck need not make Catholic assumptions about the indefectibility of the Church magisterium. The
Brazos series editors certainly did not think so. We were ecumenical in our selection of commentators. But the series can certainly
be described as "nonfoundationalist," because it does not entertain Protestant anxieties about doctrine, thinking they can be
resolved by "objective" exegesis. Doctrines can go wrong, even in
the Catholic Church—where, once defined, they are never not true
but are nevertheless sometimes misunderstood and misapplied.
Differences aside, for Catholics and Protestants alike, the church's
ongoing reform occurs in and through the never-ending work of
scriptural interpretation informed by the church's teaching and
practice. We cannot derive true doctrine from exegesis performed
without recourse to doctrine. Instead, doctrine proves itself (or
not) in its exegetical fittingness and fruitfulness.

How should we measure the fittingness and fruitfulness? In
the general introduction to the Brazos series, I cite two patristic

3. Brevard S. Childs, *The Book of Exodus: A Critical, Theological Commentary*
(Philadelphia: Westminster, 1974).

images of successful reading of Scripture. The first comes from Origen. It is an account of a tradition handed down to him by the Jewish scholar who tutored him in biblical Hebrew.

> The Hebrew said that the whole inspired Scripture may be likened, because of its obscurity, to many locked rooms in our house. By each room is placed a key, but not one that corresponds to it, so that the keys are scattered about beside the rooms, none of them matching the room by which it is placed. It is a difficult task to find the keys and match them to the rooms that they can open. We therefore know the Scriptures that are obscure only by taking the points of departure for understanding them from another place because they have their interpretive principle scattered among them.[4]

In this image, Origen urges what Brevard Childs asks us to do in his approach, which is to use Scripture to interpret Scripture. The gold standard for good interpretation, according to Origen, is an overall reading of the Bible, one that makes the best possible sense out of the extraordinary diversity of the biblical witness. For most of the Christian tradition, this overall reading tells the story of salvation from creation and fall through the covenant on Sinai to its fulfillment in Christ and his promised return in glory.

Hans Frei emphasized the narrative character of good interpretation. It's a reading of Scripture that takes us from creation through fall to covenant and salvation. But this is not the only way to conceive of interpretation that bears good fruit. The other image I cite in the general introduction to the series comes from the beginning of Irenaeus's treatise against Gnosticism, *Against Heresies* (1.8). I've used this image already in this book. Irenaeus pictures Scripture as a great mosaic depicting a handsome king. The problem rests in the fact that the individual pieces of the

---

4. Fragment from the preface to *Commentary on Psalms 1–25*, preserved in Origen's *Philocalia*, in Joseph W. Trigg, *Origen*, The Early Church Fathers (London: Routledge, 1998), 70–71.

mosaic, like the keys in Origen's image, are scattered before us. Our job is painstakingly to assemble the mosaic, putting each piece in its proper place, so that the image of the handsome king— Christ, our Lord—comes into view. As I argue in my extended discussion of Origen in chapter 3, the truest test of interpretation rests in its power to bring us to see Christ.

In his Exodus commentary, Brevard Childs also included material from the history of precritical exegesis. In this respect, he anticipated the approach found in the Ancient Christian Commentary on Scripture and the Church's Bible, two series that bring before contemporary readers selected portions of early Christian exegesis. To a greater or lesser extent, most volumes in the Brazos series engage patristic, medieval, and Reformation exegesis. But the aim of the series is to be tutored by the Old Readers. Our job is to learn from past masters. It is not sufficient to recount their readings. We must follow in their footsteps as we seek to interpret Scripture anew.

The series is unprofessional and unauthorized. In nearly all instances, modern commentary series require exegetes to be certified by the academy as "biblical scholars." The Brazos series did not adopt strict disciplinary requirements. Our aim was good exegesis informed by the church's wisdom. There are certainly biblical scholars who can do exactly that. But our academic training forms us deeply. This is especially so in biblical studies, which has a militant, boot-camp character born of a now-long tradition of fending off the demands of piety that are deemed threats to modern notions of scholarly objectivity. As a result, the series established a rule: biblical scholars could not write in their areas of expertise. Stephen Fowl, a New Testament scholar, wrote on Ruth. Christopher Seitz, an Old Testament scholar, wrote on Colossians. These two biblical scholars were exceptions. Our strong preference was for theologians and church historians. This preference flows

directly from the postliberal claim that the church's language and
practice were shaped by Scripture from the very outset.

In the early 2000s, I was circulating a number of memos among
the series editors. In one of those missives, I noted, "The series
presumes that the Christian church is a creature of the gospel."
One might say that the Christian tradition provides a "postfigur-
ing" witness to Christ in a way analogous to the Old Testament's
prefiguring. George Lindbeck's long fascination with the theme
of the church as Israel suggests something of this dynamic. In a
number of essays, he notes that the Israel of the Old Testament
provides more than a template for the church. The figuration goes
both ways. The church's history in covenant with God casts light
on the Old Testament. In Israel we see the church; in the church
we see Israel. Catholic teaching strikes this note in its own way.
The Second Vatican Council's "Dogmatic Constitution on Divine
Revelation" reiterates the Catholic claim that the church is the
custodian of a sacred tradition that is illuminated by and illuminates sacred Scripture.[5] As I've insisted from the outset, doctrine
and Scripture are intertwined. When it comes to the Bible, we
should acknowledge that those versed in the church's teaching and
formed by the church's liturgies and traditions are "native speakers" of Scripture. Putting it more bluntly: Theologians are the best
exegetes; so if you want good exegesis, hire theologians. QED.

In view of the arguments I've made in this book, the bold
claim about who is best qualified to write biblical commentaries is formally correct. But it is not very convincing in real life.
At this point in time, many theologians lack expert knowledge
in Hebrew or Greek. (I'm among the ignorant!) Moreover—and
more importantly—modern traditions of theology often lack firm
anchors in the life of the church. Our training answers to late-
modern academic culture, perhaps more so than do some forms

    5. Vatican II, "Dogmatic Constitution on Divine Revelation," *Dei Verbum* (The
Holy See: Web Archive), sec. 8, https://www.vatican.va/archive/hist_councils/ii_vatican
_council/documents/vat-ii_const_19651118_dei-verbum_en.html.

of biblical scholarship. Far from producing "native speakers" of Scripture, theology today often spins in orbits many planets removed from the Bible's radiance.

In truth, this sad fact about theology and theologians' alienation from Scripture played a far more important role in launching the Brazos series than negative assessments of contemporary biblical scholarship. One need but read a few treatises by the church fathers to recognize that reading the Bible and expounding its meaning for the church is the most fundamental of theological enterprises. It's a sign of the corruption of theology in our time that so few theologians take up this task. The Brazos series sought to address the scandal of theology without exegesis. To put it bluntly once again: The editors, all trained theologians, envisioned the series as exegetical remediation. We were prescribing the scriptural therapy very much needed in our wayward discipline.

Some biblical scholars have reacted ambivalently to the Brazos series. They worry about overreach and theological arrogance. But the postliberal thesis behind the Brazos series condemns theologians just as much as it empowers them. I have noted that doctrine proves itself by its exegetical fittingness and fruitfulness. This test can be applied to the work of individual theologians as well. One's theology is good only to the degree that it brings one to see Christ more clearly—which, as we learn in Luke 24, means that theology is good only insofar as it opens up the Scriptures. This, dear readers, is a daunting standard.

I am trained to follow arguments and analyze concepts, not to read sacred texts. But aside from Saint Paul's major letters, the Bible makes few arguments and does not operate with a settled set of concepts. Those of us trained in theology are tempted to sail away from the twists and turns of the biblical text and head toward long digressions concerning classical doctrines such as election, atonement, and eschatology. In the case of the Pauline Letters, these digressions can be fitting, for in many cases profound theological disputes about doctrine arise out of disagreements about

how to read Paul. George Hunsinger's commentary on Philippians
and Douglas Farrow's on 1 and 2 Thessalonians offer excellent
digressions into dogma that illuminate Paul for this reason. But
for most of the Bible, a "theological" approach can lead us to use
Scripture as a launching pad for theological arguments rather than
using theological arguments to enter more deeply into the text.
To apply George Lindbeck's insight to exegetical work: Scripture
absorbs theology rather than theology absorbing the text.

Did the Brazos commentary series succeed? Somewhat, in my
judgment. First, though, let's look at some failures.

Some volumes have sold well, especially those written by well-
known figures such as Jaroslav Pelikan and Stanley Hauerwas.
But the series *as a series* has not succeeded in winning the loyalty
of readers. Why is this the case?

One reason rests in the fact that the Yale School and postliberal theology flourished in a time of ecumenical optimism. After
Vatican II, Catholicism engaged Protestant theology. Protestants
read Karl Rahner, Henri de Lubac, and Hans Urs von Balthasar.
The ecumenical spirit of those years was sustained by a capacious
university culture that was no longer invested in denominational
struggles over doctrine but nevertheless included theology within
its ambit. In my lifetime, the secularization of Western intellectual
culture has accelerated dramatically. Theology has been driven out
of the university and back into the churches. To the extent that
theology remains in academic settings, it now conforms to new or-
thodoxies (feminist theology, postcolonial theology, and so forth).
At the same time, the churches have turned in on themselves, often
because of internal battles over theology and especially sex. As a
consequence, in the twenty-first century our theological concerns
have been "re-denominationalized." This phenomenon makes the
ecumenical approach of the Brazos commentary series a liability.
For which church and into which tradition do we speak?

Another reason the series has met with uneven commercial success is that it lacks a standard format. Each author is free to adopt his or her own approach. Some comment on verses. Others comment on entire chapters. Attention to philological issues varies. Some appeal to modern scholarship. Others make little or no mention of recent scholarship. As a consequence, each volume is idiosyncratic, making the overall project more a collection of volumes than a series.

Finally—and this is perhaps the most significant factor—the Yale School arose within mainline Protestantism. Its talk of post-liberal theology addressed a growing sense that the liberal theological tradition had reached a dead end. As I've noted, the Brazos series took its inspiration from the Yale School and postliberal theology. As a consequence, the series is closely linked to a tradition in American religious history that, however important in previous decades, was already waning by the time I did my graduate studies at Yale in the 1980s. It is not an insignificant fact that all the series editors are (or were) Anglicans or Lutherans. Many authors in the series are (or have been) mainline Protestants. As I write, at the beginning of the third decade of the twenty-first century, the mainline churches have been reduced to a faint shadow of their former selves. One might say that there is a sociological principle of accordance that explains why the uptake of the Brazos series has not been wide: it lacks a vibrant church audience that is in accord with its theological heritage. Such are the vicissitudes of history, which God in his providential wisdom directs.

I left my position as a theology professor ten years ago, and I no longer attend professional meetings on a regular basis. This makes me a poor judge of the influence of the Brazos series in theological circles. Nevertheless, I'll venture to say that the *idea* of the series—expressed in the rhetorically pointed general introduction—generated more discussion and debate than have the individual volumes. The November 2004 Annual Meeting of the American Academy of Religion featured a well-attended session devoted to the series. But my impression is that later volumes have not been widely reviewed or discussed by scholars. Perhaps this relative lack of notice stems from the great variety of approaches. The individual commentaries do not naturally feed into existing academic fields and conversations. The ecumenical character of the series impedes consistent engagement by church-specific organizations and publications. The academic "feel" limits the audience, ruling out discussion in general-interest Christian magazines and blogs. It is a telling fact that the magazine I run, *First Things*, has not reviewed the volumes as they appear.

Influence is always hard to measure. Nevertheless, I'll venture to say that the greatest achievement of the Brazos series has been to exist. Yale in the 1980s and then Duke Divinity School in the 1990s offered exciting prospects for theological renewal. We can add Notre Dame as a Catholic partner in this promise. Brevard Childs, Chris Seitz, and Richard Hays were biblical scholars leaning toward theology. In the late 1980s, Richard John Neuhaus organized a conference on the crisis of biblical interpretation, for which then Cardinal Joseph Ratzinger provided the lead essay, as I noted in the introduction. Around the same time, David Steinmetz argued for the superiority of precritical exegesis.[6] In the early 1990s, David Yeago defended theological interpretation in a widely read essay, "The New Testament and the Nicene Dogma," which I discussed in chapter 1.[7] There was a great deal of demand for something like the Brazos series.

At the same time, modern historical-critical scholarship was entering a new phase. During my years as a graduate student, biblical studies remained within the German Protestant tradition. It was academically informed scholarship that addressed the church. But this tradition was coming to an end, replaced by scholarship

6. David Steinmetz, "The Superiority of the Pre-critical Exegesis," *Theology Today* 37, no. 1 (1980): 27–38.
7. David Yeago, "The New Testament and the Nicene Dogma," *Pro Ecclesia* 3, no. 2 (1993): 152–64.

written for the academic community. As Michael Legaspi has put it, historical criticism became academic criticism, which means any mode of reading other than a church-oriented one.[8] Consider, for example, the academically indefensible concept of a New Testament professor. What's required now is a professor of Hellenistic religion, or a professor of ancient Mediterranean culture. The modern Protestant tradition of university-trained scholars who interpret the Bible *as* Bible is in decline. And so, looking back, we can see that the Brazos series came at an auspicious moment. Just as church-oriented theologians were clamoring for exegesis, the historical scholars were abandoning the churchly audience and its concerns.

The Brazos series has published some very good volumes of biblical exegesis. But its importance very likely rests in the fact that the series came at the right time. It galvanized and solidified a growing consensus in favor of theological exegesis. There had been jewels of theologically rich exegesis in the past. I mentioned George Horne's *Commentary on the Psalms* and William Temple's *Readings in St. John's Gospel* in chapter 1. More recently, figures of genius in the conservative Protestant churches have expounded the Bible with extraordinary post-fundamentalist élan. James Jordan offers a stellar example. N. T. Wright's extraordinary output in the first decade of the twenty-first century redeemed a great deal of the theological promise of the historical-critical tradition. But the Brazos series was the first effort to put into effect a consensus in favor of theological exegesis on a large scale, and to do so with "mainstream" academic theologians.

I suppose I would say, therefore, that the Brazos Theological Commentary on the Bible series has been a modest success, at

8. Michael Legaspi, "What Ever Happened to Historical Criticism?," *Journal of Religion & Society* 9 (2007).

least from a sociological perspective. The series translated all the talk about the need for theological exegesis into a now long shelf of volumes. But did the series succeed theologically? Do the many volumes truly open up the Scriptures?

I can answer only with my own experience. In 2008 or 2009, as I was struggling with my commentary on Genesis, I recall talking to Ephraim Radner. Writing a book on a theological topic requires you to strain to find the right line of exposition and argument. At some point, your ideas jell and the book's outline becomes clear. This does not happen when you are commenting on the Bible. Exegetes must respond to what is on the page before them. Some words invite reflection on the whole truth of Scripture. The first verse of Genesis, "In the beginning . . . ," plunges us into the prologue of the Gospel of John, which is a summary of the Christian faith. And "in the beginning" has implications for foundational doctrines. I've dwelt on the exegetical puzzles and challenges of the first verse of Genesis many times in this volume. I complained to Radner that one never gains momentum in commentary. The next passage presents new and different puzzles—and invites new and different adventures of insight.

Radner responded to my lament, saying, "Ah, yes, but that's to be expected. The Bible humiliates us." I suppose that's another way of stating a postliberal truth: Scripture absorbs the theologian, rather than the theologian and his ideas absorbing the text. No doubt I manhandled various verses in Genesis, seeking to make the Word of God serve my pet ideas and private schemes. But I can report that the book of Genesis taught me a great deal about theology. I was brought low—and happily so. I'm confident that this fruitful subordination of a theologically trained mind to Scripture was the experience of all who labored in the Brazos series. For this reason, I call the effort a theological success. In the foundry of exegesis, better theologians were forged.

ACKNOWLEDGMENTS

Chapter 1 is a revised and expanded version of a lecture given at Calvin College in March 2010 and published as "What Makes Exegesis Theological?," *Nova et Vetera* 9, no. 1 (2011): 75–90.

Chapter 2 develops material given in a lecture at the May 2006 conference on reading the Bible with and for the church, sponsored by the Center for Catholic and Evangelical Theology and Duke Divinity School. The lecture was published as "Theology and Biblical Interpretation," in *Sharper Than a Two-Edged Sword: Preaching, Teaching, and Living the Bible*, ed. Michael Root and James J. Buckley (Grand Rapids: Eerdmans, 2008), 1–21. Used with permission.

Chapter 3 is a revised version of "Origen and Spiritual Interpretation," *Pro Ecclesia* 15, no. 1 (2006): 108–26. Used with permission.

Chapter 4 expands upon a paper given at the 2003 Annual Meeting of the Society of Biblical Literature.

Chapter 5 draws together material from presentations given at the 2004 Annual Meeting of the Society of Biblical Literature, Calvin

College (2007), and Hillsdale College (2008) and published as part of my commentary, *Genesis*, BTCB (Grand Rapids: Brazos, 2010).

Chapter 6 was given as a lecture at the fall 2014 conference hosted by the Paradosis Center for Theology and Scripture at John Brown University, "Engaging the Gospel of John, Engaging One Another: Catholics, Orthodox, and Evangelicals." This lecture was published as "John 17: A Theological Reading for an Ecumenical Audience" in the conference proceedings, *The Gospel of John: Theological-Ecumenical Readings*, ed. Charles Raith II (Eugene, OR: Cascade Books, 2017). Used by permission of Wipf and Stock Publishers, www.wipfandstock.com.

Chapter 7 is a substantially revised version of a paper prepared for a meeting of the Scriptural Reasoning Project hosted by the Center of Theological Inquiry, published as "*Lawe, loue, and lewete*: The Kenotic Vision of Traditional Christian Political Theology," in *Crisis, Call, and Leadership in the Abrahamic Traditions*, ed. Peter Ochs and William Stacey Johnson (New York: Palgrave Macmillan, 2009), 169–83.

Chapter 8 expands upon a presentation given at the spring 2021 Scripture and Theology Colloquium hosted by Wycliffe College.

INDEX

precritical exegesis, 154, 161, 166
presumption of accordance, 11–13,
    15–16, 18–19, 22–24, 29, 50
  in Catholic and Protestant traditions,
    12–13, 24, 35
  definition of the, 7–9, 88

Radner, Ephraim, 153, 168
Rahner, Karl, 48, 164
Ratzinger, Joseph, ix–xi, xiii, xvi,
    37n11, 166
redaction criticism, 20, 28, 46, 74

Schleiermacher, Friedrich, 5–6, 36–37,
    155
Second Vatican Council. *See* Vatican II
Sermon on the Mount, the, 59, 101,
    148, 152
sola scriptura, 11–12, 21, 37, 109

Temple, William, 4, 167
theological exegesis, xvi, 1–30, 38
  description of, 2–3, 6, 13, 32, 38
  historical exegesis versus, 33–34, 46
  modern biblical study and, 25–29, 32,
    40, 47, 67, 109–10, 158
  non-methodological character of, 6,
    14, 30, 34
  origins of the term, 4–6
  rationale for, 24, 27, 49
theological interpretation. *See* theo-
    logical exegesis
Trinity, the, 6, 15, 35, 129

Vatican II, 10–11, 37, 48, 113, 162
von Rad, Gerhard, 30, 47, 98n6

Work, Telford, 1–2

Yeago, David, 5–7, 13, 19, 22, 153, 166